Why
Scots
Matters

Why
Scots
Matters

J. Derrick McClure

First published 1988 by The Saltire Society
in association with The Scots Language Society.

This revised edition published 1997 by
The Saltire Society,
9 Fountain Close, High Street,
Edinburgh EH1 1TF.

A catalogue record for this book is available from the British Library.

ISBN 0 85411 071 2

Designed by Mitchell Graphics, Glasgow

Printed and bound in Great Britain by Bell & Bain Limited

Contents

Introduction vii

1   *The language and its name* 1

2   *Is it a language?* 11

3   *Why it matters: as a medium for letters* . . . 25

4   *Why it matters: as a source of historical evidence* . 37

5   *Why it matters: as a means of communication* . . 49

6   *And another reason* 55

7   *What should we do?* 59

Notes 69

Further Reading 73

Introduction

THE POSITION OF SCOTS in the national life of Scotland presents striking parallels to that of Gaelic. Linguistically, each is a language closely related to, and sharing a common ancestor with, the language of another country (Scots to English, Gaelic to Irish), but with features developed in Scotland, independently and over a long period, which entitle it to the status of an indigenous national tongue. Each has, at different times, been the language of the monarchy and the government of Scotland; each is the vehicle of a long and brilliant literary tradition, enduringly productive despite adverse circumstances. Each has suffered from prejudice, misunderstanding, discrimination and outright hostility, leading in both cases to a drastic decline, especially in the present century, in its numerical strength, its range of uses, and its social status.

The states of the two languages are not comparable in all respects, however; and the most important difference between them is one which operates in favour of Gaelic. Though Scots lays claim to the national adjective, it has never been universally recognised as a national language, or as a language at all. In the struggles of both tongues to avoid submergence by the common enemy, English, Gaelic has at least had the advantage of being able to confront it on, in one sense, equal terms: Gaelic is undoubtedly a distinct language. Scots has all too often been perceived as a mere dialect, which in popular thought means an inferior or corrupt form, of English: an aberration which any self-respecting person would naturally wish to avoid. It will be the intention of the present book to demonstrate the inappropriateness of such a view: to explain what Scots is, and why it matters.

One
The language and its name

To THE QUESTION "Why does Scots matter?", a sceptic might begin by retorting "What are you calling 'Scots'?". And this issue must be faced at the outset of our discussion. The everyday speech of many people in Scotland is neither English (even Scottish-accented English), Gaelic, nor any immigrant language: so much is obvious. But what precisely is the status of this speech form; and how, if at all, does it deserve to be identified by the national adjective? These questions can best be answered by a summary examination of the linguistic history of Scotland.

Long before the final breakdown of Roman Imperial rule in the province of Britannia, pirates from the North German coast had been conducting hit-and-run raids on its south-eastern littoral: the Imperial government had even been forced to appoint an official known as the Count of the Saxon Shore, responsible for coastal defences. With the collapse of Roman power in the early fifth century, Britannia fell prey to concerted attacks from the seafaring raiders; and despite a protracted and heroic resistance, led for a time by the Christian warlord who was later to acquire legendary status as King Arthur,[1] the Britons were gradually pushed westwards, while the marauding tribesmen won themselves kingdoms in the southern and eastern parts of the island. Two and a half centuries after the Imperial government's abdication of responsibility for the defence of Britannia, the Heptarchy was established: a group of seven kingdoms (though in reality the number fluctuated somewhat) covering the area from the Forth to the Channel except for Wales, Cornwall and (for a time) Cumberland. (The duration of the British resistance, incidentally, makes nonsense of the Anglocentric tradition in terms of which a phase in the island's history called "Roman Britain" is neatly followed by one called "Anglo-Saxon England".) The most northerly of these kingdoms was Northumbria, which straddled the present-day national boundary and occupied the region from the Humber to the Forth.

The language of the defenders was Celtic, that of the invaders

Germanic. According to the Venerable Bede, Britain was settled by
three distinct peoples, the Angles, the Saxons and the Jutes, whose
new domains were respectively the Northumbrian and Mercian
kingdoms, the four states with names ending in *-sex,* and Kent. This
is, in fact, doubtfully authentic: Bede himself uses the terms
Angle and *Saxon* as if they were completely interchangeable; and certainly the invaders shared a common language and culture. The
tongue which they spoke is now referred to as Old English or Anglo-
Saxon. The former term is preferred by some on the grounds that the
language is the direct ancestor of present-day English, and the line
of descent from it to the contemporary language is readily demon-
strable by the abundant surviving evidence; the latter by others on
the grounds that the enormous changes in the language from the
seventh century (when it first appears in written form) to the twentieth, especially the massive French influence which has made
English look so unlike the closely-related Dutch and German, make
the suggestion of recognisable similarity implied by the use of the
same name inappropriate and misleading. The invaders' own name
for it was *Englisc*. And from its earliest attestations, *Englisc* shows
varying regional forms. This was formerly explained by the assumption that the Angles, Saxons and Jutes came to the island speaking
slightly different forms of their common language; and it is still customary in philology to refer to the Mercian and Northumbrian
dialects as "Anglian" in contrast to the "Saxon" forms of further
south. More recently, the suggestion has been made that the different dialects emerged after the settlement of Britain, rather than
before it.[2] For whatever reason, at no time in its history does Anglo-
Saxon appear as a homogeneous language. (In this respect it con-
trasts strikingly with Old Irish; but the case of Anglo-Saxon is far
more typical of early written languages.) The first specimens of
written Northumbrian, which include some of the earliest records of
Anglo-Saxon, differ – not vastly but significantly nonetheless – from
those of the neighbouring kingdom of Mercia; and the dialects of the
Saxon kingdoms show features not found in either of the forms
recorded from the northern parts of the Heptarchy. It is not to be
imagined, of course, that each of the seven kingdoms possessed a
single consistent dialect, with clearly-marked linguistic boundaries
at the frontiers: such a situation is in practice never found, and
is least of all to be expected in the political and demographic

instability of the seventh and eighth centuries. Nonetheless, it is clear that the Anglo-Saxon tongue was spoken in forms which varied from one end of its domain to the other.

One of the first and most striking literary records of northern Anglo-Saxon is carved in stone, on the splendid decorated cross at Ruthwell in Dumfriesshire. This is a set of fragmentary quotations from *The Dream of the Rood*, a poem on the Crucifixion which is one of the masterpieces of Anglo-Saxon literature. The Ruthwell Cross was carved around the turn of the seventh and eighth centuries, at which time Dumfriesshire was not yet in Scottish hands; however, it is pleasing to observe that one of the earliest records of a major literary text in Northumbrian Anglo-Saxon, the ancestor of the Scots tongue, is found within what is now Scotland.[3]

Meanwhile the North of Britain had suffered its own invasion. Gaelic-speaking tribesmen from Ireland, called by the Romans (but not by themselves) *Scoti,* had established themselves in what is now Argyll, and in other settlements, though these did not prove durable, in Cumbria and Wales. The language of these settlers was again Celtic, but a different form of Celtic from that of the Britons. Gradually the Gaelic tongue – identical then, and for many centuries to come, with the language of Ireland – spread eastwards across the Mounth, penetrated Carrick and Galloway, and even reached into what is now the Lothians and Borders. Here, its speakers came into contact with the Anglo-Saxons of Northumbria: among the relatively few Gaelic place-names in South-East Scotland the significant Achingall, "field of the foreigners", suggests that by the time Gaelic speech reached this area the Anglo-Saxons were already in possession.

The North-East was the domain of the Picts.[4] The unique artistic achievements of these people, including stone and metal artifacts of a quality unsurpassed in Dark Age Europe and certain unexplained symbols and motifs not found elsewhere, and their success in resisting both Roman and Saxon attempts at conquest, have always appealed to the popular imagination: their language and culture gradually yielded, however, to that of the Gaelic-speaking Scots, who possessed the advantage of literacy. (Old Irish, the modern name for the language which the Scots spoke, was by a long way the first European tongue to develop a written literature after Greek and

Latin.) When the Vikings began their depredations on the British
Isles, the resultant eastward shifting of the Gaelic power-base
appears to have led to a close military and dynastic alliance of Picts
and Scots, culminating in the acquisition of the Pictish throne by the
Gaelic king Kenneth MacAlpin in 843.

The Kingdom of Scots and Picts thus formed was called Alba, and
its dominant language was Gaelic. To the Anglo-Saxons it was
known by its Latin-derived name of Scotia or Scotland, though in
the Anglo-Saxon tongue "Scotland" at this period also meant
Ireland. The term *Scot*, that is, is at first associated with the language and civilisation of the Gaelic people, and not with the Anglo-
Saxon-derived speech which today bears the name *Scots*.The origin
of the word *Scot* is a historical puzzle: it was not the native name of
any early people, and its source in Latin is undetermined. More to
our purpose, however, and indeed essential to appreciate, is the significant change in the application of the name during its recorded
history.

Besides their artistic and cultural achievements, the Scots and the
Picts had been dynamic and resilient peoples, participating to the
full in the hectic and bloodstained power-play of Dark Age Britain.
The united monarchy of Alba continued this tradition, embarking
soon after its foundation on a policy of southward expansion. The
South-West was annexed in the late ninth century; and shortly
thereafter first the fortress of Dun Eideann or Edinburgh, and sub-
sequently the entire Lothian area down to the Tweed, fell into
Scottish hands. Malcolm II's victory over the Angles at Carham in
1018 confirmed what was already a *de facto* Scottish hold on this
Saxon-speaking territory. The Kings of Scots had thus acquired a
new appanage foreign in language and culture to their kingdom, and
one which was only loosely integrated with it for a long time to
come. To such imposing Celtic warrior-kings as Malcolm II
(1005–34) and his grandson Macbeth (1040–57), it would hardly
have seemed likely that the language of Lothian would eventually
usurp the place of Gaelic as the principal language of the kingdom.

The sequence of events which led to this began in the reign of
Malcolm III (1057–93), the king whom Shakespeare, following
sources which treat historic facts in a cavalier fashion, shows tri-
umphantly acclaimed King of Scotland after his victory over
Macbeth. A series of sweeping reforms, aimed at strengthening the

monarchy by reorganising it on Anglo-Norman lines, was instigated by Malcolm and brought to completion in the reigns of his sons, most notably the admirable David I (1124–53); and these reforms had not only the desired effect of greatly enhancing the prosperity and political stability of Scotland but the presumably unforeseen one of increasing the importance of the Anglo-Saxon tongue. The most important innovation was the introduction of burghs. The burgh, a settlement with legally defined commercial rights and privileges, was an Anglo-Norman concept; and its associated vocabulary of quasi-technical terms such as *craft, gild, alderman, toll, gate* and *wynd*, is largely Anglo-Saxon. The fairs and markets held in the burghs, and the system of baronial courts which made them centres of justice, entailed the conducting of business principally in that language, since the institutions themselves were imported from Anglo-Saxon-speaking territories. Gaelic-speakers from the hinterland, coming to the burghs to trade or to litigate, would have found it advantageous to acquire at least a basic knowledge of the new tongue. The actual number of Anglo-Saxon-speakers was increased: by refugees fleeing into Scottish territory from the iron rule of William the Conqueror and his son, or the anarchy of Stephen's reign; and by others who came in response to the kings' deliberate policy of encouraging immigration and granting land on easy terms to the incomers. The language of these incomers was in some cases Dutch or Flemish, or Scandinavian, as their numbers included arrivals directly from these countries and from communities settled in England; but those people would naturally adopt Anglo-Saxon, closely related to their own tongues, rather than Gaelic.[5]

Anglo-Saxon, then, was associated in Scotland almost from the start with attractive new developments in trade and commerce, with enterprise and with prosperity. And a remarkable feature of the process is the ease with which it seems to have been accomplished. The traditional picture of Scotland as split between Gaelic-speaking Highlands and Scots-speaking Lowlands, antipathetic and irreconcilable, is derived from a later age: the late eleventh, twelfth and thirteenth centuries showed, on the whole, a surprising lack of hostility among Scotland's various peoples, and the almost steady growth of a strong and benevolent feudal monarchy. There was no question as yet of Anglo-Saxon becoming the official language of the kingdom, or claiming the name "Scots"; yet when David I and his immediate successors addressed charters to "all the peoples of the realm, French, Angles, Scots and Gallovidians" – meaning respectively the landowning families of Norman or Anglo-Norman origin, the Anglo-Saxon-speakers of the South and East, the Gaelic-speakers of the West and the central hinterland, and the mixed peoples of the extreme South-West – it is significant that the new culture appears to take precedence over the old.

What ensured the triumph of the Anglo-Saxon tongue, and ensured also that this would be overtly at the expense of Gaelic, was the dying-out of the Celtic royal line in the persons of Alexander III (1249–86) and his grand-daughter, the Maid of Norway, and the passing of the throne to three Lowland families, the Balliols, Bruces and Stewarts. Donald, Lord of the Isles, supported Robert Bruce in his struggles against English aggression: his successors, however, by pursuing a more devious policy, made of the Lordship virtually an independent sovereignty, sometimes an ally but more often an avowed enemy of the King of Scots. The monarchs, for their part, began to identify themselves with the Lowland rather than the Highland part of their kingdom. The principal seat of government was moved from Perth to Edinburgh, in the heart of the Anglo-Saxon-speaking territory. When James I (1406–37) had the Acts of his predecessors translated from Latin into the vernacular it was the Lowland tongue, not Gaelic, that he used; and the many legislative proceedings of that energetic monarch were conveyed to his subjects in the same language. Already in the reigns of Robert II (1371–90) and Robert III (1390–1406) the Lowland tongue had begun to show promise as a language of poetry: under the Jameses it became one of the most brilliant literary vernaculars in Europe. Kings, lords, and commoners, clerics and laymen, were now utilising the Anglo-Saxon speech of the Lowlands; and though Gaelic continued to be spoken over more than half the land area of Scotland, and to be the vehicle of the ancient, vigorous and highly distinctive culture of the Highlands, it was through the medium of the Anglo-Saxon tongue that Lowland Scotland played its part, and no inconsiderable part, in the mainstream culture of European Christendom.

The language, however, was known as *Inglis*. Even such ardently patriotic writers as John Barbour and Blind Harry saw no incongruity in referring to their language by the name of their people's mortal enemies. Yet there is nothing surprising in this: the native name *Englisc*, slightly altered in form, had simply continued in use as the regular term for Anglo-Saxon speech throughout its domain. The Scots, too, were perceptive enough to realise that the language of their enemies had in the hands of Chaucer, Gower and Lydgate developed an outstanding vernacular literature; and the Scottish writers, by proclaiming that they used the same language as those great masters, were in fact staking a claim on their own behalf to be contributing to the literary tradition which they represented.

It was in the late fifteenth century that the practice of calling the language by the national adjective arose; though it did not, and indeed never has, become universal. The first major writer (though not the first of any kind) to insist that *Scottis* was a distinct language from *Inglis* was the poet Gavin Douglas; and indeed he seems to have wished to make a special point of it, arguing in the Prologue to his great translation from Virgil that, just as Latin borrowed terms from Greek, so he, to enrich his Scots, was sometimes obliged to employ loans from Latin, French *or English*. Douglas was not necessarily motivated in this by political or cultural patriotism: other writers whose credentials in this respect were far sounder than his had been, and would be, content to refer to their language as *Inglis*. But Douglas had spent some time in England, and his laying emphasis on the differences between Scots and English was probably a recognition of the linguistic fact that by now the two tongues, despite their common origin, had diverged so considerably as to merit the titles appropriate to distinct national languages.

The importance of Douglas's bold proclamation of his tongue's right to the name *Scottis* should not be underrated. It demonstrates a fundamental change in the national self-awareness. In the Scottish realm which had been founded by Gaels such as Macbeth and Malcolm II and III, and moulded into a nation-state by Normanised Gaels such as David I and the three Alexanders, the Anglo-Saxon language and its associated culture were now central. The original *Scoti* had been Gaelic-speakers, in Latin texts *lingua Scotica* and *lingua Scotorum* had always meant Gaelic, and even in the vernacular the language of the Gaels of ancient times had been referred to as *Scottis* – though the customary name for *contemporary* Gaelic speech was *Irisch* or *Ersche*. (This latter usage, incidentally, is at least as justifiable as that of *Inglis* for the Lowland tongue, for until the six-

teenth century the language of the Highlands, in its literary form at
any rate, was not only related to but substantially identical to the
language of Ireland.) Now, by contrast, the Lowlanders had appro-
priated the national adjective for their tongue: by implication claiming to be the people in whom Scottish nationality was most clearly
demonstrated. Douglas, apart from his literary genius, was a fairly
typical representative of his class and his time (that is, he was ambi-
tious, self-seeking and politically devious); and, although he did not
persuade the entire population of the Lowlands to adopt the name
Scottis in contradistinction to *Inglis*, his usage was not a mere idiosyncrasy; and shortly afterwards the name came into widespread
use.[6]

This, then, is Scots: the language brought within the boundaries
of what is now Scotland by the encroaching Germanic invaders in
the sixth century, becoming one of the languages of the Scottish
king's domains in the eleventh, gradually establishing itself as the
medium through which Scotland became a fully-fledged European
state in the twelfth and thirteenth, finally coming to be employed as
the language of monarchy and government in the early fifteenth, and
all the while diversifying from the related dialect of the English
metropolis.

Its steady growth in social and cultural importance, and in linguistic and literary sophistication, was, alas, not maintained. Gavin
Douglas, the first writer of European stature to insist on its distinctive status, is himself one of its greatest practitioners then or since:
many critics have argued that in his *Eneados* Scots reaches a level of
subtlety and expressiveness which no subsequent writer in the language has ever achieved. That the *Eneados* was completed in the
year of Flodden is not without significance: the catastrophic loss of
not only the gifted and popular James IV (1488–1513) but almost
the entire Scottish nobility was bound to lead to a period of political
chaos and decline in the national cultural life. Gavin Douglas himself, drawn into the murky field of politics by the marriage of his
nephew to the Queen Dowager, wrote no more after 1513. The
active reign of James V (1513–44), a vigorous but wilful and erratic
monarch, only partly fulfilled its promise of national recovery; and,
following his early death, a new threat to the integrity of the Scottish
tongue grew apace: the Protestant reform movement in the Church.
The Reformers – not, it would seem, deliberately, but simply lacking

any sense that the distinctiveness of Scots was to be particularly prized – undermined the language by their use of English for their Confessions of Faith,[7] the importation of works by English theologians, and above all the introduction of the Geneva Bible. The success of the Reformation imposed on Scotland a theocracy increasingly hostile to artistic expression of any kind: this is the main explanation for the fact that, while in England the art of drama was enjoying its most splendid efflorescence since classical Athens, Scotland failed totally to develop anything comparable. And the role of England in abetting the Scottish reformers – Henry VIII, the government of Edward VI, and later Elizabeth giving them both overt and covert help as a convenient and effective means of subverting order in Scotland – ensured that with the triumph of Protestantism English cultural and political influence would become dominant and the nation's traditional links with France and other European powers would be weakened or broken.

The traditional role of the monarch as a patron of letters and hence a support for Scots as a language of poetry was ended at a stroke by the departure of James VI for London in 1603. James, a king whose remarkable talents and achievements have been obscured by the prevalence of a caricaturing image derived from hostile English criticism,[8] had tried deliberately and with some success to establish his court as a haven of poetic activity; but the enriching effect of this on the language and its culture vanished with the loss of the court. The growing familiarity with London on the part of Scottish men of culture after 1603, and still more after the Union of the Parliaments in 1707, led to a gradual adoption of English as an alternative to Scots. In the period of national regeneration after the disastrous decades preceding and immediately following the Union of Parliaments, the magnificent period of achievement which earned for Edinburgh the nickname of "the Athens of the North", the fashionable use of English among the educated classes was taken much further, some even attempting to excise all Scots features from their speech. And the schools, in recent times aided by radio and television, have always been inclined to present English rather than Scots as a model for the speech of children. The practice of stigmatising the language as merely a debased form of English, begun in the eighteenth century, is still very much with us.

Yet throughout its vicissitudes Scots has remained obstinately
alive. Many writers have deliberately tried to develop it as a medium for letters, scholars and concerned laymen have argued for its
preservation, and (most important of all) the mass of the populace
has simply continued to use it as their ancestors had done, in everyday speech. And in the Scotland of today, when Walter Scott's observation that "the peculiar features of (the nation's) manners and character are daily melting and dissolving into those of her sister and ally
(*sic*)"[9] is as true as it was then, the maintenance of our national
tongue is a matter of urgency.

Two
Is *it a language?*

Many people who regard Scottish vernacular speech with affection and even pride, as well as many who treat it with contempt, are reluctant to acknowledge that it deserves to be called a *language*. It is, rather, a "dialect" – or else it is simply "bad English". It is genuinely difficult to discuss this question, much more to resolve it, because of the nebulosity of the terms. There is in fact no single criterion which can be applied in all cases to decide whether a given speech form may be classed as a language; and of the various factors which can be considered, not one provides an unambiguous answer in the case of Scots.

That it is "bad English", certainly, is a notion which may be dismissed from the start. What this phrase appears to mean is often something like "a carelessly or clumsily mangled version of standard literary English spoken by people who are too lazy, ignorant, perverse or whatever to speak it properly". At the very least, it assumes the existence of a "good English" which the guilty speakers are trying and failing to achieve. Nothing could be more inappropriate than to regard Scots in this light. As will already be clear, Scots has as long a pedigree as English; and a speech form which generation after generation has acquired and used as a mother tongue is nobody's faulty attempt at anything. "Bad English" in this sense is what is spoken by, let us say, an adult foreign learner with an imperfect knowledge of the language, making mistakes which he presumably would avoid if he could: Scots, a speech form existing in its own right, is not to be likened to this.

The status of a speech form as dialect or language is inescapably relative. To a native speaker of English it is obvious without discussion that Gaelic is a distinct language: *vis-à-vis* Irish, the position of Gaelic is by no means so certain. A standard work of Celtic philological scholarship, T. F. O'Rahilly's *Irish Dialects Past and Present*,[10] includes a chapter on Scottish (i.e. Scottish Gaelic), discussing it comparatively with the Gaelic dialects of Ireland. The language relative to which we have to determine the status of Scots is, naturally,

English. Certainly Scots is not *a* dialect of English, for Scots itself is not uniform but shows considerable local and social variations; but are the dialects of Buchan, Fife, Shetland, the Glasgow conurbation and other areas to be considered as being in the same category as those of Yorkshire or Devonshire?

The situation is further complicated by the fact that Scots in its classical form – the real-life counterpart to what A. J. Aitken has ironically styled "Ideal Scots"[11] – is not to be found everywhere. More frequently met with are speakers whose Scots contains a substantial, if in many cases varying, number of English words and phonological forms. (Such people are to be distinguished from the full bilinguals who can switch consciously between Scots and Scottish Standard English, of whom there are many in areas, such as Aberdeenshire, with a distinctive and well-preserved local dialect.) We will return to this issue later: for the present let it be accepted that in examining the right of Scots to be classed as a language, the reference is to a maximally differentiated Scots. To the argument, should anyone wish to offer it, that such an exercise has no practical value as the speech form under discussion is virtually extinct, one answer is a direct denial of the premise: there are speakers, and in greater numbers than is sometimes realised, whose command of the full riches of their regions' traditional vocabulary and idiom would dispel at once any doubts regarding the independent status and enduring vitality of Scots; and another will be suggested in the final chapter.

Two useful concepts introduced by the German scholar Heinz Kloss may illuminate the discussion. These are *abstand* and *ausbau* languages.[12] The first suggests "difference" or "disparity", and refers to the degree of mutual resemblance between two speech forms. Two tongues which are unlike to the extent that a monolingual speaker of one would find the other very difficult or impossible to understand are *abstand* languages: English and Gaelic, or French and German, are obvious examples. *Ausbau* refers to the degree of functional development of a language: the concept will be discussed later.

In attempting to apply the *abstand* criterion to more closely-related speech-forms, several difficulties arise. There can be no question that a monolingual from Toronto or Sydney if suddenly transported to a Glasgow factory or an Aberdeenshire farm would find himself out of his depth linguistically, but such a crude test is of very little value: the same would probably be true if he were confronted with a group of broad Cockney- or "Brum"-speakers. Mutual intelligibility may be asymmetrical: it is observable that when Scottish and American children play together the latter show difficulties of comprehension which the former do not – of course, for the simple reason that American accents are regularly heard on television in Scotland whereas the reverse is not the case. Other factors than the purely linguistic may influence reactions to modes of speech: social attitudes, aesthetic feelings, or simple personal prejudice. In the late 1950s, the BBC departed from its policy of employing only broadcasters with South-Eastern English accents, and engaged an announcer (June Imray) who spoke, not any form of Scots, but standard English with a North-Eastern Scottish accent. This provoked what seems in retrospect to have been an extraordinary amount of controversy, in the midst of which an indignant English listener complained to the BBC that she "needed an interpreter" to understand Miss Imray's words. This, of course, was nothing but a particularly silly and graceless example of linguistic snobbery; yet it is indicative of the fact that ignorance and prejudice may very easily influence an individual's perception of even slightly unfamiliar speech forms. The complaints regularly made of the "unintelligibility" of the dialects heard when the BBC broadcasts a Scottish documentary or a dramatisation of a Scottish literary classic are largely on the same level, and are of no importance as linguistic evidence. Clearly something less variable and more objective than the reactions of individuals must be cited in testing a language for *abstand* status.

It is universally known that Scots and English show regular correspondences in the pronunciation of cognate words. Where English-speakers say *town, down, mouse, house, out, about* and so on, Scots-speakers use forms with the vowel of French *fou*. To English *go, whole, home, more, bone, stone* correspond Scots *gae, haill, hame, mair, bane, stane*. The vowel often written *oo* in English has different counterparts in the various Scots dialects: *moon, goose, tooth, roof* correspond to what is often spelt *muin* etc., and pronounced *min, mane, meen* or *meun* (with a vowel resembling that in French *deux*) in different parts of Scotland.[13] Words with *a* in English often have in their Scots cognates *e*: *bress, gress, gless, efter, gether, Setterday*; when the vowel is followed by an *r*-sound, the Scots word usually has an *ai*: *fairm, hairt, pairt, hairst* (cf. *harvest*). An *o* in English, especially when followed or preceded by a *p, b* or *f*, often corresponds to an *a* in Scots: *aff, laft, saft, pat, drap, sang, lang, wrang*. A similar correspondence of sounds (this time not reflected in the spelling) is seen, though for a different reason, between the English and the Scots forms of *want, wash, wasp, water*: in English pronounced with an *o*-vowel, in Scots with *a*. Where English words have the diphthong *oi* their Scots counterparts generally have the *i*-sound of *line*: *jine, ile, pynt, bile, spile*. Many English words have an *l* which is missing from their Scots cognates: to *fall, call, all, gold, golf, hole, pull, wool* correspond (in the spelling preferred by many recent writers) *faa, caa, aa, gowd, gowf, howe, pu, ou*. Likewise the *v* of some English words is absent in Scots: *hae, gie, ower, loe*. Consonant clusters are often simplified in Scots: *fac, connec, expec*; *lann, finn, enn, grunn, thunner, wunner, caunle, haunle*. And, of course, Scots makes use of a consonant sound long since vanished from English in *nicht, lauch, teuch, troch, dochter*. These are only some of the most widespread characteristics of Scots speech (and of course all could be exemplified by many words other than those cited): each of the various regional dialects has its own features of pronunciation, of which a full listing – only a tiny sampling will be given here – would run to many pages. In the North-East, initial *wh*- becomes *f-*: *fit, faar, fan; fite, funn* (whin), *fussle*; the vowel in words of the *hame*-group is raised to *ee* when followed by *n*: *been, steen, aleen*; a characteristic *w*-glide appears in *gweed, cweel, scweel*; and the *ew* in words like *new* becomes an *ow*-like diphthong: *neow, feow, deow, beowty*. The famous *yow an mey* of Hawick is an example of a general tendency in Border dialects (except where the Tweed forms the frontier) to diphthongise final *ee*- and *oo*-sounds: *how, now*, and *cow* (but not *brown!*) are pronounced as in English, rhyming with the local pronunciations of *through, dou* (dove) and *pu* (pull); and not only *me* but *he* and *we*, and also words like *wee, see, free, tree* and so on, have the *ey*-sound. Also in the Borders, "home" is not *hame* but *hyim*: the only example still in common use of a once widespread change by which *yits* was heard for *aits, yick* for *aik, hyil* for *haill*. The Northern Isles have dialects characterised by, among many other things, a use of *t* or *d* where both English and most other forms of Scots have *th*: *trou, tank, aert* (earth); *dis, dat, dou, dee* (thou, thee: the use of these pronouns is still retained in the Isles); *blyde, meed* (*meith*, "landmark"); a fricative *ch* (i.e. as in *nicht*) instead of the *k*-sound in the sequence *qu*: *chwick, chween, chwestion*; and (in Shetland but not in Orkney) the reduction of initial *ch* (as in church) to *sh*: *shair, sheese*.

It may well be true that the historic differences between the dialects are gradually lessening. Not only is English making inroads into the integrity of the spoken varieties, but several local forms are giving place to a general Scots: it would be hard to find anyone in Buchan who still says *snyaave* and *byaave*, but the forms now heard are *snaa* and *blaa*, not *snow* and *blow*; a Borderer whose grandfather said *hyill* no longer says that, but he does not say *whole*: he says *haill*. Nonetheless, enough of the old distinctions are preserved for the existence of regional dialects to be still a very potent feature of the Scots linguistic scene.

It is probably fair to say that most people, other than language scholars, vaguely imagine these Scots pronunciations to represent distortions or corruptions of the contemporary English words. Even what purport to be textbooks on Scots, or at least serious reference works, often resort to such phrasing as "English *a* is replaced by *e* in words like *bress, gress* ..." But nothing could be more misleading. These divergences are the results of the centuries of independent development that separate Scots and English from the common ancestor, Anglo-Saxon: they are evidence of historical change; and it is essential to realise that language change is simply a fact, and neither necessarily good nor necessarily bad in itself. The tendency of the nineteenth and early twentieth centuries to see language change as "progress" is as unmeaning as the previously fashionable view that it represented "corruption". A fundamental tendency to diversify is simply natural to language as it is to species of living organisms. Anglo-Saxon has fragmented to produce English and Scots, both existing in various dialect forms, just as Old Irish has given rise to the several extant (and several lost) dialects of Scottish and Irish Gaelic, and Latin to seven contemporary national languages and numerous speech forms of lesser status. Sometimes Scots has preserved a more conservative sound feature where English has diverged more radically from the ancestor language: the retention of the monophthong in the *toun, hous* words (diphthongised in English during the sixteenth century) and of the fricative in *nicht* and *thocht* (already beginning to disappear in Southern England by the late mediaeval period), and the preservation of the *a*-sound suggested by the spelling of *water* and *warm*. (The adoption of an *o*-like vowel was a late change in English, not accepted as standard until the eighteenth century.) Sometimes it is English that shows the greater conservatism: the Scots loss of *l* and *v* and the simplification of consonant clusters, all attested in the spellings of late-mediaeval Scottish texts, have simply not happened in England. Sometimes a change which was at least incipient in both countries has been fully established in Scots but not in English: there is evidence that pronunciations such as *drap* and *jine* were in widespread use, even in "polite" circles, in England in the sixteenth and seventeenth centuries;[14] but, probably because of the influence of the spelling, they never became generalised as in Scotland. And in many instances, both languages have diverged, but in different directions, from the common ancestor: neither *home* nor *hame* is very close to the Anglo-Saxon word *ham*; the vowel in English *good* and the very different vowels in its various Scots cognates all represent independent developments of the Anglo-Saxon *god* (with the vowel of *go*). Several of the characteristic changes affecting Scots can be parallelled in the history of other languages: French has lost the *l* of Latin after certain vowels, as in *autre, coup, poumon* (cf. Italian *altro, colpo, polmone*); Gaelic in some dialects has lost a *v*-sound in medial and final position (in *leabhar, gobhainn, sabhal,* the *bh*, representing an earlier *v*-sound, is now mute); the reduction of *nd* to *n* in words like *end* and *land* is also characteristic of Norwegian and Danish. Certainly the independent phonological changes which have affected Anglo-Saxon in the north and in the south of its domain from its earliest history are numerous and extensive enough to have led to massive differences between Scots and English.

An interesting method of assessing the degree of difference between languages by comparison of their basic vocabularies has been proposed by the American linguist Morris Swadesh.[15] This method utilises a list of 100 concepts fundamental to all human cultures: people, animals, and their body parts; food items, elementary numbers, weather conditions; and categorises the relationship between two speech forms by the extent to which their words for these concepts coincide. The theoretical presumption on which Swadesh's system is based, that the core vocabulary of a language if unaffected by outside influences changes at a constant rate, is probably unwarranted and certainly unverifiable; but the results of applying the test can be quite striking. Many of Swadesh's hundred basic concepts would be expressed by identical words in English and Scots: *bird, tree, egg, kill, walk, fire*; and many others by phonological cognates, which for this approach are not classed as different words: *bone-bane, head-heid, earth-yird*. However, in some cases a well-known Scots word unrelated to the English at any rate *could* be cited: *big-muckle, small-wee, person-body, ear-lug, grease-creish* (not related, despite their similarity, but borrowings from different words in Old French), *nose-neb, claw-clook, belly-wame/kyte, neck-craig, smoke-reek, mountain-ben*. In Swadesh's terms this results in an 89% coincidence between the basic vocabularies of Scots and English; and according to him, the coincidence between Czech and Slovak, German and Dutch, and Danish, Norwegian and Swedish, are in all cases over 90%. Certainly not much weight can be put on this result; yet it does show that a form of Scots can at least be conceived of which is less closely related to English than Norwegian is to Danish.

Besides pronunciation and vocabulary, the grammar of Scots also shows differences from that of English: fewer and less striking than in the other two aspects of the language, but significant nonetheless.[16] Some of these are shared with many other speech-forms apart from standard literary English: the emergence of a second person plural pronoun *yous*; the retention of a triple distinction between *this, that* and *yon* which in English has been reduced to *this* and *that* (though the forms *thir* as the plural of *this, thae* of *that*, and the assimilated *thon* instead of *yon*, are distinctively Scots); the loss of distinction between past tense and past participle (*I done it, we havena went*); and the use of double negatives (*ye never telt me naethin about it*). (Scots, however, has a more idiomatic usage of juxtaposing two negatives which operate independently: *He isnae still no workin; It's no that I've been no gaun oot wi her, I jist havenae been out wi her!*).[17] Others are more characteristically Scots. The uses of the definite article differ from English: *He's got the cold, the flu; he's at the scuil, in the hospital, awa tae the kirk*. Prepositions vary in application from their English counterparts: *better o a rest, get chased fae the*

polis, feart for the dug, waitin on his frein. In verbs, an -s ending is regularly used in other forms than the third person singular: James
Hogg's "When the kye comes hame" is a perfectly grammatical line
in Scots, and everybody has heard the "... an she says ... an I says ..."
which punctuate neighbourly exchanges of news. A distinction is
possible between a first-person form with and without the -s ending:
"When I gae hame I'll tell him" – "When I gaes hame I aye maks
mysell a cup o tea". Auxiliary verb constructions sometimes differ
quite strikingly from English: *he'll no can manage, they used tae could
dae it, they micht no would like tae come wi us.* The verb *be* is often
omitted after a demonstrative: *here a sweetie tae ye, there the bus ower
thonder.* There is no sense in describing these usages as "ungram-
matical": this simply means that they do not conform to the
grammar of standard literary English, and as they are *not* standard
literary English there is no reason why they should; and readers who
bristled at the *I done it* examples in particular, as probably many did,
might take note of Robert Henryson's "A woful wedo hameward is
he went" and Robert Fergusson's "Ye wha are fain to hae your name
Wrote in the bonny book of fame . . ."[18]

As a final point regarding the *abstand* status of Scots, it may be
noted that the absence of a systematically-devised spelling system
for the language has resulted in its being written, from the seventeenth century to the mid-twentieth, with a slightly modified form
of English orthography, and thus being made to *look* much more like
English than it actually is. Recent experiments by Scots writers have
gone at least some way towards rectifying this anomaly:[19] unquestionably the second of the two following passages gives the impression of being written in a distinct language in a way that the first
does not, though if read aloud by a competent Scots speaker both
would sound equally Scots. (Many people have been heard to say
that they find Burns easier to understand from a written text than
from hearing his poems recited.)

> There wad aiblins nane o' you ken Marion. She lived i' the Dod-Sheil; and had
> a callant to the lang piper, him that Squire Ridley's man beat at the Peel-hill meet-
> ing. Weel, you see, he was a gilliegaupy of a callant, gayan like the dad o' him; for
> Marion said he wad hae eaten a horse ahint the saddle; and as her sheiling wasna
> unco weel stored o' meat, she had ill getting him mainteened; till at the lang and
> the last it just came to this pass that whenever Jock was i' the house, it was a con-
> stant battle atween Marion and him.[20]
> About twa hunder yeir syne, the war a puir man that wrocht on a ferm in

Lanarkshire. He wes whit is kent as an "orraman"; that is ti say he haed nae kynd
o raiglar wark set out for him, but wes expekkit ti turn his haund ti whitevir wes
needfu.

    Ae day, his maister sent him out ti kest peits on a bit muirland that wes pairt o
his ferm. This muir run up at the ae end til a craig wi a byordnar maik. This wes
kent as "Merlin's Craig", kis the warlok haed aince bidden thare langsyne; or sae
the kintrae fowk said.[21]

Ausbau—the name literally means "build-up", and suggests
"development" or "consolidation" – refers to the degree of independent linguistic development which a language can show. An *ausbau*
language is one which has been adapted for a wide range of uses,
and one language has *ausbau* status relative to another if their ranges
of functions are mutually comparable. In this there can be no possi-
bility of measuring Scots against a world language like English, with
an accepted application, in both its spoken and written forms, to all
branches of human activity: not only conversation and literature,
but non-literary writing such as treatises on scientific and technical
subjects, legal, commercial and business documents, instruction
manuals, advertisements, official forms, and the multifarious other
uses which form part of everyday life in a modern technological
state. Scots, clearly, has developed part of the way towards this
stage, but not all. It has a written form and possesses a splendid corpus of literature, including poetry, fictional dialogue, narrative prose
and drama, but the extent to which it is used for non-literary writing is negligible, despite some experimental attempts to employ it
for literary criticism and linguistic discussion. One only has to
imagine a quality newspaper, containing reports and analyses of
local, national and world politics, editorials, sports commentaries,
reviews of books, theatre and broadcasting, and the other regular
features of *The Scotsman* or *The Herald* written entirely in Scots, to
realise how far it is from the *ausbau* level of a world language. That
it could, in theory, be developed for all these purposes is not in question: the relevant fact is that at present it is not. However, one need
not insist that only speech forms with the range of application of
English or French can qualify as languages by the *ausbau* criterion.
To do so would eliminate at a stroke all but a numerically tiny group
among the world's four or five thousand extant languages. Africa,
South and Central America, Indonesia and Australia contain hundreds of indigenous languages which have only the beginnings of

written literature, or none at all; nearer to home, the Celtic languages, and even those of some of the smaller European states, have
limited or negligible use in fields of advanced learning. And Scots is
far more extensively developed towards *ausbau* status than any other
Anglo-Saxon-derived speech-form except standard literary English
itself. No dialect of England, for example, or recently-formed
English-based pidgin or creole, is remotely comparable to Scots in
the extent and quality of the literature produced in that tongue since
mediaeval times.

   Abstand and *ausbau* status are conferred on a language by linguistic facts. Other factors may operate, however, in determining the
view held of a speech form. Two tongues which are to a considerable
extent mutually intelligible may be classed as different languages
because they are spoken under different flags. Scandinavian languages provide an example of this. Speakers of Norwegian, Danish
and Swedish can communicate with each other without serious dif-
ficulty; and the practice of distinguishing three languages – or four
if the two official forms of Norwegian are classed separately – is
entirely due to the fact that the ever-fluctuating number of Scandinavian kingdoms has settled for the present at three. Portuguese is
sufficiently close to Spanish for its speakers to find Castilian quite
readily intelligible (though communication in the other direction is
less easy); and because of the accidents of linguistic geography, the
tongue spoken in the region of Spain on the north bank of the River
Minho, Galician, is closer to Portuguese than to Castilian. And the
suggestion prompted by this line of argument that Scots was a language till 1603 or 1707 and thereupon became a dialect is not as
absurd as it may sound. In the early sixteenth century Scots was
incontrovertibly an *ausbau* language. It also had claim to being an
abstand language: the Spanish ambassador at the court of James IV
reported to his master that the King's Scots was as different from
English as Aragonese (i.e. Catalan) from Castilian.[22] By any linguistic criterion, that is, Scots in the fifteenth and sixteenth centuries
was a distinct language. But though the loss of political independence did not *automatically* bring about any change in the position
of the language, still less in the language itself, it prepared the
way for such changes to take place. Even after 1603, and 1707,
Scots could have retained its status as a full national language – had
its speakers so desired. And this is the crucial factor. There are many

instances of tongues which objectively have no better claim than Scots to *abstand* or *ausbau* status gaining international recognition as languages; but in all such cases it is because their speakers regard them, and make strong and conscious efforts to promote them, as such. Thus the Norwegians, on gaining independence, vigorously embarked on the task of differentiating their language from Danish; and though the attempt to establish "new Norwegian" as the sole national language has not been entirely successful, even Norwegians who prefer the "Dano-Norwegian" of the period before independence would forcefully repudiate any suggestion that they were simply speaking Danish. Thus Dutch-speaking Belgians often prefer to call their language Flemish, to counter any impression that they are speaking a language not of their own country, though it may in reality be closer to the Dutch of the Netherlands than to the genuine Flemish dialects; and what is in effect Dutch in another guise, Afrikaans, has been developed as an official language in South Africa. Thus Catalan, in Spain regarded as a dialect, is cherished as the national *language* in the tiny state of Andorra; and held as a language also by many Spanish Catalonians on such grounds as its distinctiveness from Castilian, its possession of a literature, and its importance as a mark of Catalonian identity. But the language of Lowland Scotland has never been seen by the populace as a whole – only by some individuals – as a national symbol or a focus for patriotic pride. Even after the term *Scottis* was introduced, many people still adhered to the practice of calling it *Inglis*, the same term as they used for the language of England. When Scots in the sixteenth and seventeenth centuries was confronted in its homeland with the social and cultural prestige of English, a determined language loyalty could perhaps have preserved it; but that was not to be found, or not on a large enough scale. Ramsay, Fergusson, Burns, Walter Scott, Hugh MacDiarmid and his successors, all tried in different ways and from somewhat different motives to establish a national pride in the Scots tongue, but their success in this respect was only partial.

It is because of this general absence of any conception of Scots as a distinct speech-form, unique and proper to the Scottish nation, that the language failed to maintain its integrity; becoming progressively intermixed with English in the speech of individuals, coming to be regarded (increasingly, as a result of the last-named

factor) not as an autonomous tongue but as a faulty attempt at
another.   This is why the speech regularly heard in Lowland
Scotland today is not often the traditional dialects in their pristine
purity but more usually an erratic and inconsistent mixture of Scots
and English.   This, too, is why speakers of Scots rarely evince a
strong feeling of national pride in the language: some, as a result of
school and parental conditioning, are somewhat ashamed or embar-
rassed at it, some regard it with a nostalgic or antiquarian interest,
many at best feel a *local* pride in their Buchan or Border tongue; but
a clear feeling that Scots could or should be developed as a part of
our national identity is not widespread in Scotland. Yet it is important to realise that this situation is neither new nor unique. In the
early eighteenth century, bilingualism in Scots and English was
already commonplace among all classes: Robert Burns's father, for
instance, was locally reputed for his ability to speak excellent
English. Charles Keith in the eighteenth century and Logie Robertson in the nineteenth are among the poets who have called attention
to what they saw as the diminishing fluency in Scots among the
populace in general.[23] And in other countries, speech forms of comparable status to Scots, because of prolonged contact with a dominant language, exist in a variety of forms varying from conservative
dialects to what is virtually the dominant language with a local
colouring: a close parallel is Frisian, influenced to a greater or a
lesser degree, and differently in its rural and its urban forms, by
Dutch.[24]

To the concepts of *abstand* and *ausbau* languages may be added a
more recent one, introduced by another German scholar Dietrich
Strauss, of *apperceptional* languages.[25] Two speech-forms are apperceptional languages if their speakers, or even the speakers of only
one of them, regard the differences between them as a matter of
importance and of pride. The Czechs and the Slovaks, for example,
are historically different peoples – the present writer was once
warned by a Slovak colleague that he would react to being called a
Czech as the writer would to being called an Englishman – and
though the linguistic differences between Czech and Slovak are very
slight, their distinct identities were insisted upon even during the
temporary political union of the two peoples (from 1918 to 1993) in
a state called Czechoslovakia. The establishment of an apperceptional difference may be the first step in the development of a

language to *ausbau* status, as appears to be happening with Afrikaans: the founding of separate Czech and Slovak republics has also been the signal for writers and scholars in both countries, but especially Slovakia, to develop the languages on deliberately diverging courses. Lowland Scots is a contrary case: at the time when it most surely merited both *abstand* and *ausbau* status it was not, or was only showing signs of becoming, an apperceptional language; and it has never truly attained to being one. From this point of view, the question whether Scots is a language must be answered: to the extent that its speakers do not *think* of it as a language, it is not one.

The status of Scots continues to stimulate controversy: in the correspondence pages of our national newspapers, for example, the debate surfaces every year or so with the regularity of the revolving seasons. From one point of view this could be seen as encouraging: for as long as the nature and status of Scots remains a live issue, the language itself is alive and occupying the attention of the public. Yet from another, the unending rehearsal of the same arguments is profoundly distressing. First, it reveals the excessively simple terms in which the issue is popularly seen. Contributors to the debate almost invariably appear to believe that some day an argument will be found (or that such an argument exists and they are now producing it) which will prove once and for all that Scots really *is* a language or really *is* a dialect. There is no such argument, for there is no simple two-way choice between "language" and "dialect" as the status of a speech-form: those terms have no clear-cut definition and the opposition between them is almost wholly factitious. If this chapter has demonstrated anything at all, it has surely demonstrated that. The American sociolinguist Joshua Fishman, by examining speech-forms for the presence or absence of the four features *standardisation* (possession of a canonical set of rules for spelling and grammar); *autonomy* (state of being regarded by its speakers as an independent speech form rather than assessed with reference to an external standard); *historicity* (state of having a long and continuous record of development as a living tongue); and *vitality* (state of functioning as the everyday means of communication for an identifiable community), is able to distinguish no fewer than seven classes of speech-form: standard language, classical language, artificial language, vernacular, dialect, creole and pidgin – and Scots cannot be incontrovertibly categorised even in terms of this schema, as the features of standardisation and autonomy are partial or incipient rather than simply "present" or "absent". (The presence of the other two features in Scots can hardly be questioned.)

Second and more important, the terms in which the debate is conducted often betray with ominous clarity the assumption that the linguistic status of Scots should condition our attitudes to it or our practices and policies concerning it. Whether stated overtly, implied, or (seemingly) simply taken for granted, the idea which underlies much of the debate is that Scots should be given official recognition, accorded a greater degree of social acceptability, encouraged as a field of study and as a medium of education, and so on, *if and only if* it can be proved to be a "language". This assumption is patently absurd even on its own terms, since the practice of according these marks of recognition to a speech-form is in itself one of the things that determine that speech-form's status as a "language" or as something else. Besides, it can all too readily serve as a superficial rationalisation of what is ultimately nothing but the familiar inculcated prejudice against Scots: the notion, perpetuated by a long tradition of miseducation, that it is simply "bad English". In popular thought, "dialect" has a derogatory ring, and many people who seek to prove that Scots is a "dialect" are at a deeper level merely seeking to justify the continuing neglect and disparagement, and ultimate disappearance, of Scots as a spoken tongue.

Unquestionably Scots was once a language; unquestionably it has the potential to become one again. But to make it so is not only, perhaps not even principally, a matter of changing the tongue itself, but of changing its speakers' attitudes towards it. Popular impressions can be changed; and when they are mistaken impressions, it is a matter of importance that they should be. The task of those who are concerned for the future of Scots is to persuade the Scottish people that we have, as a unique national possession, a highly distinctive and expressive tongue which is also the vehicle for a literature of great antiquity, merit and durability. And if we wait until we have "proved" Scots to be a "language" before embarking on this task, we assuredly never will.

Three
Why it matters:
as a medium for letters

SPEAKERS OF ENGLISH have traditionally prided themselves on sharing the language of Shakespeare, Milton, Wordsworth, Dickens and so on. By the same token, speakers of Scots may, and should, take pride in a language which has been the medium of some of the great figures of European literature.

To claim *The Dream of the Rood* as an early Scottish poem would be an excessive indulgence in patriotic pride; and after the probable date of this poem there is a gap of over five hundred years before any considerable literature in the Anglo-Saxon tongue of Scotland comes to light. A few scraps, such as a gibe at "Edward with his lang schankis", a doggerel celebration of Bannockburn (well enough known in England three centuries later for Christopher Marlowe to quote it in his *Edward II*), and the well-known lament for the death of Alexander III, are all that remains of Scots literature before the late fourteenth century. Yet we know that much has been lost, even from this early period. Thomas the Rhymer is a historical figure, notwithstanding his immortalisation in a fairy ballad; and he is probably to be identified with the Thomas who composed an epic poem on Sir Tristram. And the first extant major work in Scots, it could be argued somewhat impressionistically, is too fine an artistic achievement not to have emerged from an already well-established tradition.

Whatever its precedents, the piece which opens the pageant of Scots literature could hardly be more dramatic in itself nor more appropriate as the beginning of a national poetic tradition. It is an epic account of the life and military achievements of Robert Bruce, composed by John Barbour, Archdeacon of Aberdeen, in the reign of Bruce's less distinguished grandson Robert II (1371–90). The *Brus* is many things: a major source of historical information, a textbook of mediaeval warfare, a lifelike portrait of a king who, though neither impeccable nor infallible, emerges as on any showing one of the great figures of the European Middle Ages, a thrilling tale of heroic adventure. It is also the first and in some respects the finest treat-

25

ment of several themes which recur in Scottish literature and life: patriotic pride, confidence in the God-given right of the Scottish nation to maintain its integrity, and above all a sense of the "community of the realm": of Scotland as belonging to, even consisting of, not only the ruling classes but the common people. To describe this sentiment as democratic would of course be an absurd anachronism; but again and again in Scottish literature, from Barbour onwards, the dignity of the common man and the close inter-relationship of the various ranks of society recurs as a principle.

In grammar and orthography Barbour's language is not grossly different from that of his contemporary Chaucer, though naturally their poetic practices are very unlike: Barbour probably regarded himself as a historian rather than a poet, and his style is much less ornate and more utilitarian than that of his English colleague. But his vocabulary contains several words unattested in English texts,[26] and details of spelling and grammar show that the independent development of Scots as a language has unmistakably begun.

The next major literary work in Scots is more remarkable for quantity than for quality: Andrew of Wyntoun's *Original Cronikyl of Scotland* (c.1420) relates the country's history from the Creation to Wyntoun's own day. As literature, his massive opus is mostly pedestrian stuff compared to Barbour's lively narrative; but besides its historical interest, it demonstrates the growing confidence of Scotsmen in their vernacular tongue: the normal medium for a large-scale historical narrative in the early fifteenth century would still have been Latin.

A few other works, such as a noteworthy anonymous collection of saints' lives, also belong to the early Stewart period; but it was when the pallid and melancholy figures of Robert II and Robert III gave place to the flamboyant Jameses that the Scots tongue entered its outstanding period of literary efflorescence.[27] In the two hundred years from the death of Robert III in 1406 to the Union of the Crowns in 1603, each of the seven reigns is adorned with the poetry of at least one figure of international stature, in a procession as colourful, varied and fascinating as that of the Stewart monarchs themselves. James I (1406–37) was a gifted poet in his own right. His *The Kingis Quair* (despite longstanding controversy, there is no serious reason to doubt the early attribution of this poem to James) is an intricate and beautiful work in which events from the King's early life form a background to a searching philosophical discussion, couched in allegorical terms, of love – courtly and Christian, human and divine – and of the status of free will in a divinely-ordained world. With James's polished and elegant style, strongly contrasted with the plain vigour of Barbour, Scots becomes a fit vehicle for an intellectual and sophisticated courtly poetry. To the short reign of James II (1437–60) belongs *The Buke of the Houlat* by Richard Holland, a strange and intriguing piece containing a fund of esoteric lore and a pointed commentary on the Scottish and European politics of the time, woven with remarkable skill into the framework of a bird fable. In this and other alliterative poems of slightly later date, still another string is added, so to speak, to the Scots poetic lyre: Holland combines the rugged rhythms of the native stress-timed metre with a colourful and innovative vocabulary. The next reign was the *floruit* of Blind Harry (no other contemporary name is known for him), whose epic *Wallace*, though far less historically accurate than Barbour's *Brus*, matches it as a realistic and gripping tale of war and transcends it in imaginative scope by elevating its hero to the status of a divinely-appointed martyr to the cause of Scottish independence. Robert Henryson (?1430–1500) was the greatest of the mediaeval Scottish poets and arguably the greatest poet in Europe of his century; in his work the Scots tongue in its full expressive range conveys his poignant vision of the wholesome and appealing qualities of human life tragically unprotected in a hostile world. If Henryson is the most profound of Scots poets, William Dunbar, James IV's court poet, is the most brilliant: Scots, varying from its most elegant and mellifluous to its most harsh and vulgar tones, is for him the medium for poetry of unsurpassed technical virtuosity.

The progressive literary development of the Scots tongue, and its enrichment by borrowings from French and Latin and by the verbal inventiveness of the poets, reached its peak in the work of Gavin Douglas, whose *Eneados* ranks among the great translations of European literature. Douglas was keenly aware of the audacity of his venture in translating the *Aeneid* into his "bad harsk speche and lewit barbour tung", and in a vigorously-worded prologue he explains and justifies his principles as translator; but the real justification of his effort is the result: the transformation of Virgil into a

Scots epic in which the many variations of mood and style in the original are counterpointed in a display of outstanding verbal skill. In a wider context, Douglas's achievement signals the final triumph of a revolution in attitudes to vernacular literature: neither in Scots nor in any other spoken tongue had any previous writer ventured on a complete poetic translation of one of the most universally admired of classical poems.

Douglas's work may represent the high-water mark of the development of Scots as a poetic language, but it was some time yet before a visible decline set in. David Lyndsay (1490–1555), the principal literary figure of James V's reign, was not only a prolific poet but a gifted dramatist, whose *Ane Satire of the Thrie Estatis* shows his fine command of the rhetorical possibilities of Scots and his taste for its adaptability to sardonic earthy humour. Alexander Scott, who follows in the procession, is associated with Mary's reign by an elaborate poem of advice which he addressed to her; but he is best remembered as a song-writer whose lyrics, mostly on the theme of love, show a technical skill excelled only by Dunbar. Alexander Montgomerie surmounts – if occasionally with a struggle – the challenge of couching a lengthy political and philosophical allegory (*The Cherrie and the Slae*) in a complex and difficult verse form. Montgomerie is sometimes called the last of the Makars (the name given collectively to the great company of mediaeval Scottish poets); but this sequence appropriately closes with James VI, for a time Montgomerie's patron, who used Scots for prose works on a variety of topics in which logical argument, fiery rhetoric and a very unexalted shrewdness combine in varying proportions; as well as being no contemptible poet in the Italian- and French-derived modes then in fashion.

The works of the Makars from Barbour to Montgomerie show the development of Scots to a literary language of unlimited range and flexibility. The contrast between the mellifluous Latin- and French-derived words used in dignified registers and the noisier, more consonantal music of the native word-stock had made possible a wide variety of sound-patterns; and those, together with the tongue's enormous vocabulary and potential in both the cadences of Latinate rhetoric and the pithy and snappy expressions of vernacular speech, had been exploited with superb skill by the poets. Their language is not hopelessly unlike ours today; and to readers with even an unsystematic knowledge of modern Scots it would be little more difficult to read than English literature of the same period – with at least some of which it is still assumed that every educated person in Scotland as well as England has an acquaintance.

In the work of the Stewart poets, what is worthy of remark is the power and range of their Scots: not the fact that Scots was their medium. *That* is a matter of course: they wrote Scots as Englishmen wrote English or Frenchmen French, because it was the native vernacular of their country (or of their part of it). Following the departure of James VI, this could never again be said. The King himself, and the court poets who accompanied him southwards, quickly adopted English as their literary language: even William Drummond of Hawthornden, the only major poet of the reign to stay in Scotland after the Union of the Crowns, chose for his medium a language indistinguishable in its written form from English. It may be that the sounds which he intended the English spellings to represent were those of Scots: this does not alter the fact that the integrity of the written Scots tongue was now gone. Distinctive Scots features of vocabulary and grammar are very rare in Drummond.

For most of the seventeenth century, literature in Scots was notable for neither quantity nor quality. The few writers to employ the language that had been Henryson's were content with a limited vocabulary, a grammar wavering inconsistently between Scots and English, and an ambiguous orthography which failed utterly to indicate the Scots pronunciations. And when a full canon of Scots began to make its voice heard again in the eighteenth century, several things had changed. First, Scots poets could no longer realistically draw on the resources of Latin and French to adorn their language in its more elevated registers. Scots was not now the medium through which Scotsmen approached the culture of Europe – and that in itself, of course, no longer bore any resemblance to the Christendom for which Henryson and Dunbar had written. Second, Scots could no longer be used in the unselfconscious manner of the mediaeval poets, for bilingualism was now a fact of Scottish life. Most educated Scotsmen could, though it is not to be imagined that they generally did, speak English, and all were accustomed to reading it. And English was considered a more polite language than Scots. To write in Scots, therefore, was an act with overt and inescapable cultural, even political, implications: a deliberate

•

gesture of support for a denigrated tongue. Third, the current of Scots letters had run very thin for a long time, and contact with the great mediaeval tradition had been largely lost. Barbour, Harry and Lyndsay remained popular, but not the other Makars: Henryson and Dunbar, for example, would have been widely known only through the selections from their works, in some cases distorted by idiosyncratic editing, which appeared in Allan Ramsay's *The Ever Green*. What the poets of the eighteenth century had to draw on, besides their own ingenuity and their native knowledge of the language, was the fine tradition of folk literature and folklore which had never ceased to flourish in Scotland, and which proved a fertile source of inspiration. The influence of the ballads – not only those circulating in broadsheets and in collections such as *The Ever Green* but the hundreds known purely through oral transmission – is readily visible in much poetry of this period.

The poets of the Vernacular Revival, as the eighteenth-century movement is called, at their best produced works not unworthy of their mediaeval predecessors. Allan Ramsay combined a neat skill in flyting and in satire, a rare but genuine lyrical gift, and a propensity for ale-house humour, in the most influential corpus of poetry that any single poet in Scotland, at least until MacDiarmid, ever produced. Robert Fergusson, gifted with a deeper human sympathy and a greater linguistic skill than Ramsay while sharing in his robust and genial conviviality, found new subtleties in the Scots tongue; and resorted to Anglicisation far more rarely than either his lesser precursor or his greater successor. Robert Burns combined the literary influence of Ramsay and Fergusson with that of the folk poetry in which he had been steeped since childhood to produce a Scots as multi-faceted as his own extraordinary personality. While Ramsay, Fergusson, Burns and many lesser writers were reviving Scots poetry in the central and southern parts of Scotland – Burns's Ayrshire in particular was a positive hive of poetic activity – the first writers in what was to become a great North-Eastern tradition were appearing: Alexander Ross in his delightful pastoral epic *Helenore* showed that a Scots with a decided flavour of Aberdeenshire dialect was a viable poetic medium (though a century was to pass before any other poet rose to the challenge of writing in a strongly-marked local dialect), John Skinner produced one song, *Tullochgorum*, which aroused the enthusiastic approval of Fergusson and Burns, and Andrew Shirrefs developed the satirical and vituperative side of Scots poetry to a fine art.

All these poets were of course aware of the availability of English as an alternative poetic medium to Scots. Fergusson distinguished clearly between his poems in Scots and his poems in English; Ramsay and (with greater skill) Burns often combined the two in individual poems to mark changes of mood or stages in the train of thought. The fact that Scots was no longer the sole language of non-Gaelic Scotland was not without its literary advantages: without sacrificing the range or the force of their Scots, the finest poets of the eighteenth century could, by incorporating English as well, draw for literary effect on the different tones and different implications of the two tongues. The enormous influence of Ramsay, however, and the fact that he personally happened to have a much greater gift for original and memorable verse in Scots than in English, established a tradition of reserving Scots largely for the genres in which he most excelled – satire, comedy and pastoral – and leaving other poetic modes to the dominance of English.

In the early nineteenth century, a new literary use of Scots, fictional dialogue, was brought to its full glory in the works of Walter Scott. He was not the first novelist to make Scottish characters speak in Scots: Tobias Smollet had already done so; but Scott's many memorable characters – Andrew Fairservice, Edie Ochiltree, Cuddie Headrigg, Jeanie Deans, Caleb Balderstone, James VI – demonstrate the splendid vitality of the Scots tongue and of the people whom he could remember, or observe, using it. Many writers of fiction have followed Scott in dialogue. John Galt's strongly Ayrshire-accented voice enhances the social and psychological realism of his memoir novels; James Hogg's Border dialect is sometimes distinguishable among the remarkable variety of linguistic effects which he achieves through the medium of Scots; George MacDonald, in the domestic novels which are (undeservedly) among the neglected parts of his large and diverse oeuvre, shows how an uncompromising Aberdeenshire Doric can express the full range of human emotions; William Alexander makes his characters discuss momentous social and political issues, with an eloquence worthy of the strength of their commitments, in the same dialect; J. M. Barrie's sometimes deplorable sentimentality is redeemed by his masterly handling of Angus speech; J. J. Bell's lightweight but shrewdly-observed scenes of childhood in Glasgow employ a Scots with at least some flavour of the city dialect; George Douglas Brown, another Ayrshireman, enlivens his character-studies by giving each of his fictitious personages not only the local dialect but individual idiosyncrasies of speech as well. R. L. Stevenson combines an impeccable knowledge of vernacular Scots with lyric and dramatic gifts which make of him the finest exponent of the medium after Scott.

Scots prose continued to develop throughout the nineteenth century, in the hands of not only gifted novelists but, in the second half of the century, a whole school of local journalists who used the vernacular for fiction and also for articles and features on politics, agriculture, social developments and items of local and national news. Ephemeral though most of their writings were,[28] they ensured that Scots played an important and dynamic part in the life of the nation, not only as a language of conversation but as the vehicle for a popular intellectual culture based on the written word. Scots poetry, by contrast, in this period suffered a serious decline: not in quantity, as in the seventeenth century, but in quality. A drearily unimaginative reliance on repetitions of Burns's themes and verse-forms, in a language which was often little more than a diluted version of his, is all too characteristic of much nineteenth-century poetry. In 1887, however, R. L. Stevenson published a volume of well-crafted poems in a Scots which showed a richer vocabulary and more inventive phrasing than any poet had achieved since Burns's death; and shortly afterwards Charles Murray began producing poems of enormous popular appeal, depicting Aberdeenshire scenes and characters in the dialect they would have spoken. The contrasting techniques of Stevenson and Murray may be seen as marking the first stage in a development which has proved most stimulating in Scots letters from then till now: a split between what might be called a national and a regional branch in Scots writing. The former employs a language not associated with one region of Scotland as contrasted with others, drawing its vocabulary from different parts of the country and from earlier literature; the latter utilises the dialect of one clearly defined locality, carefully representing its distinctive grammar and pronunciation, and drawing on the local setting and way of life for inspiration. Murray was succeeded by a line of poets, some of at least equal gifts, who developed for the North-East the finest tradition of dialect poetry (it already had the finest tradition of folksong) in mainland Scotland. Other localities have likewise produced impressive collections of poetry in their local tongues: those of the Northern Isles, especially Shetland, vie with Aberdeenshire in quality; the Borders, Fife and Galloway have their local bards; and a remarkable recent development has been the emergence of the working-class vernacular of Glasgow, a despised dialect to which some people would even deny the title of Scots, as a potent vehicle for experimental literature. Stevenson, for his part, was followed by Pittendreigh MacGillivray and Lewis Spence, neither a major poet but both, particularly the latter, interesting for their experiments with quasi-mediaeval language; and then by the outstanding figure who single-handedly revolutionised the Scottish literary scene, Christopher Grieve or Hugh MacDiarmid.

Grieve's contribution to the literary development of Scots began with a series of lyrics whose merit is in no way lessened by the fact that several are patently showcases for a striking word or phrase, and continued with some extended metaphysical rhapsodies in which the language is not only handled with an imaginative skill equalled in Scotland only by the two or three greatest of his predecessors, but shown to be capable of sustaining flights of intellectual speculation rarely attempted in its earlier history. Grieve's "synthetic Scots", so-called from his practice of augmenting his native Border dialect by extensive and conspicuous use of words gathered from reference works, was adversely criticised for its artificiality; but the quality of the poetry he produced in it is ample vindication of his method. And the viability of this constructed language was promptly confirmed by a remarkable group of gifted poets who, while strikingly different from each other in their individual personalities and poetic voices, shared with each other and with their master a lively interest in linguistic experimentation, a determined commitment to the cause of restoring Scots to the place it once held as a major literary language, and an incisive, hard-hitting, intellectual approach to their subjects contrasting totally with the sentimentality of most nineteenth-century Scots poetry.

William Soutar, the most traditional of the company, brought a heightened emotional and imaginative force to long-established lyrical forms; Sydney Goodsir Smith, taking the watchword "Back to Dunbar" more literally than MacDiarmid ever did, found a remarkable vitality in Middle Scots words and word-formations; Robert

Garioch experimented with registers varying from quasi-mediaeval aureation to Edinburgh back-green vernacular; Alexander Scott handled an idiosyncratic mixture of North-East dialect, literary Scots of the past and contemporary slang with truly amazing technical skill; Tom Scott imparted a ruthless intensity to his visionary poetry by his selection of potent Scots words; Douglas Young made expressive and often witty use of a sometimes recondite vocabulary in an opus which includes Scots translations from at least ten languages; and Alastair Mackie, also a gifted translator, used a Scots with a strong Aberdeen flavour to evoke life's trials with realism and compassion. These outstanding poets, and many lesser figures, have collectively revitalised literary Scots (often known as Lallans) to an extent that would have seemed inconceivable in the first quarter of the present century. Post-MacDiarmid Lallans is often remote from vernacular speech – of the seven major poets mentioned Alastair Mackie's language is probably the closest to, and Douglas Young's the furthest from, anybody's actual spoken Scots – but the use of such a medium is fully justified by the results: no reader who is prepared to make the effort required to overcome the initial unfamiliarity of their language can deny its enormous expressive power. Not only poetry but prose and drama have in recent decades been produced in Scots; Robert McLellan is the most outstanding figure in both these fields, but he is by no means alone: Alexander Reid and Robert Kemp in drama, James Robertson and Sheena Blackhall in short stories, spring to mind among the writers who have expanded the range of Scots into those hitherto infrequently-attempted genres. William Lorimer's magnificent translation of the New Testament, an achievement parallelled in Scots letters only by Gavin Douglas's *Eneados*, may be seen as the ultimate confirmation of the renewed status of Scots as a fully-developed literary language.

The use of Scots for fictional dialogue continues apace, many writers showing no less energy and imagination than their predecessors. A traditional Scots based on the long-established rural dialects is still often to be found: a notable exponent is Fionn MacColla, who in his novel of the Highland Clearances dramatises the conflict by contrasting the Gaelic-accented speech of the Highlanders with the dense and powerfully rhetorical Lowland Scots of the Factor. An interesting development, however, in prose as in poetry, has been the increasing use of urban dialect for novels of the industrial working class (latterly the post-industrial workless class). This movement was launched in 1935 with *No Mean City*, A. MacArthur and J. K. Long's enduringly popular, if flawed, novel of the Glasgow gangland, and later developed by highly individual novelists such as George Friel, William McIlvanney and James Kelman. Younger short story writers, such as Matthew Fitt, John Murray and William Hershaw, continue to develop a Scots based firmly on contemporary demotic speech but with admixture in varying degrees of literary and even poetic vocabulary. Perhaps the most radical exponent of today's spoken Scots is the phenomenally popular Irvine Welsh, who uses a brutally accurate representation of Edinburgh gutter-talk in his merciless evocations of the city's underworld of drugs and petty crime.

In the field of drama, a notable recent development is the presence of a number of small touring companies performing new and experimental plays, many on social and political topics, in which Scots (literary and colloquial) is used extensively. This movement may be said to have begun with the founding of the 7:84 company in 1973 and its drama of Highland history *The Cheviot, the Stag and the Black, Black Oil*: among the most remarkable of its recent products is *An Gaisgeach*, a dramatic re-interpretation of Macbeth, with dialogue in a mixture of literary Scots, Aberdeenshire Doric, Gaelic and English (the last for the character of Malcolm!).

At the time of writing, Scots letters continue in a vigorously healthy state. MacDiarmid's influence, years after his death, is far from spent: the last of the giants among his immediate successors, Tom Scott and Alastair Mackie, died in 1995, but younger poets are continuing to experiment in both synthetic Scots and dialect writing. Even a mere list of names for the most interesting among the new generation of poets would be disproportionately long, and what follows is an almost random selection: Tom Hubbard's classically disciplined literary Scots, W. N. Herbert's exuberant celebrations of Dundee demotic, Harvey Holton's Fife-accented lyricism, Tom Leonard's and Alison Kermack's scathingly witty exploitation of phonetically-spelt Glaswegian, Robert Crawford's more elaborate but no less forceful cantrips with the same dialect, Sheena Blackhall's wide-ranging explorations of the expressive force of Aberdeenshire Doric. Stories and plays appear regularly (the magazine *Lallans* making an important contribution as an outlet for the former); and experiments have been made in applying the language to literary criticism and other academic writings: this is not, at least as yet, a fully-established field for Scots writing, and not all of the experiments in it have been convincing, but a few articles in Scots have appeared even in scholarly publications with international readerships.[29]

Perennial controversies regarding the tongue's potential ranges of style, idiom and function ensure that the field remains lively and stimulating. So too does the ongoing debate on its spelling; there is no "standard" orthography for Scots, and the point is often made that this is an advantage in facilitating the kaleidoscopic variety of regionally and socially diversified dialects used in literature; but several writers and scholars, most notably David Purves, have argued that a canonical form with agreed rules for grammar and spelling, used not necessarily to the exclusion of the dialects, would enhance the status of Scots and increase its chances of international recognition. What their efforts have so far proved, for good or ill, is that it is much easier to devise a practical and academically creditable orthography than to persuade people to use it.

Scots matters, therefore, to the extent that anyone unfamiliar with it is ignorant of one of the most distinguished of Europe's smaller national literatures, and one of the most exuberant branches of the contemporary literary scene.

Four
Why it matters:
as a source of historical evidence

Scots, as we have seen, had its origin in Northumbrian Anglo-Saxon. Its historical development from the ancestor language reflects in interesting ways the history of the nation.

The most important factor in raising the status of Scots at the expense of Gaelic was the founding of the burghs. It is therefore appropriate that the earliest vernacular Anglo-Saxon words to be recorded in Scotland are nearly all connected with the new system of community organisation and landholding: names of burghs or landmarks with reference to which a settlement or holding is located, or terms relating to community life or to local government and laws.[30] These words first appear in Latin documents such as charters, acts of parliament and burgh or abbey records, some dating from centuries before the beginning of extant vernacular literature: they may gloss Latin words or be incorporated in the Latin text, sometimes, entertainingly, with Latin endings – "arbitrium aldirmanni et feryngmanorum". Aldeburgh, Bradeford, Blakeburn, Kaldestrem are place-names in the Anglo-Saxon tongue, readily comprehensible, with very early attestations. Topographic terms such as *haugh* (low-lying arable land), *law* (hill), *lech* (marsh), *cleugh* (gorge or ravine), *faugh* (fallow land), appear as common nouns or place-name elements: all survive to the present day in the latter use if not in the former. *Burgh* and *burgess* are themselves Anglo-Saxon terms; so are the names of officials in local government such as *alderman* (now an English and not a Scottish term, but frequently attested in early Scottish texts) and *farthingman* (the "feryngmanus" of the quotation above: a uniquely Scottish term for a guild officer). *Thane,* a title (which Macbeth assuredly never bore) for a minor royal official, is simply the Anglo-Saxon word for a king's retainer. Some intriguing Saxon-derived legal terms appear: *bludewit* (action for bloodshed); *heregeld* or *herieth* (a payment made to a landowner on the death of a husbandman tenant, of the dead man's best animal); *inborch* (security paid on behalf of a Scot held for debt in England: the converse was *uteborch*); *infangthefe* (the right

37

of a lord to try one arrested for theft on his own land); *birthinsake* (the theft of goods that could be carried away on one's back – such, presumably, as a sheep or a sack of grain – for which, incidentally, the punishment, as defined in a later translation of the relevant Act of Parliament, was "to be weil dungin or his ere to be schorn").

Apart entirely from the specialised terminology of the burghs, many of our distinctive Scots words today are of Anglo-Saxon derivation: that is, they have simply survived in the Scots language – and in some cases, as a glance at the Linguistic Atlas of Scotland will demonstrate, also in northern English dialects – from early times to the present day. We have noted how frequently a Scots word and its English cognate illustrate different developments in pronunciation from the original Anglo-Saxon forms: in the following cases an original vocabulary item has been retained in Scotland whereas its nearest equivalent in English is a different word which may not be of native origin at all. Such are *bairn* (child), *bide* (stay, live), *byre* (cowshed), *bield* (shelter), *blate* (shy), *deave* (deafen), *dicht* (wipe), *dwine* (dwindle or fade away), *greet* (cry), *gloaming* (twilight), *thrawn* (really the past participle of *thraw* [throw], which, in the sense of twist, from its frequent application to a grimace or facial contortion resulting from pain, anger etc., came to mean obstinate, perverse or sullen), *smeddum* (a popular word among modern writers, originally meaning fine powder but having come to mean something like "resourcefulness, courage in adversity, strength of character").

Lowland Scots and Gaelic have of course been spoken together in the same realm since Scots first emerged. The traditional antagonism of Highlanders and Lowlanders is by no means a fabrication of romantic fiction writers: it was a very real part of Scottish life for many centuries; but in the high Middle Ages relations between the two sections of Scottish society were on the whole more peaceful than they later became, and many Gaelic words were adopted by the Lowland tongue.[31] Among the oldest are toponymic terms such as *bog, ben, glen, inch, loch, strath*. (The first of these has made its way into English too, probably from Irish rather than Scottish Gaelic, but only since the sixteenth century: it is first attested in Lowland Scotland in the early thirteenth.) As with the old Anglo-Saxon words cited, some Gaelic topographical terms of great antiquity survive only in place-names: *drum, tom, knock, mounth*. Gaelic gives some legal terms attested in early Scottish feudal charters but not surviving to our own days: *cane* (a tribute paid in goods), *cro* and *enach* (terms cited only once in a puzzling Act of Parliament of *circa* 1200 stating that any man's *cro, enach* and *galnys* (this is a Welsh term) are the same: all appear to be some form of blood money, fines paid to the king's officer or to a man's kin as compensation for a murder or injury); *tanist,* the appointed successor to a high king, and *davach,* a measure of land.

Other Gaelic-derived words, much more widely known than those, are *kelpie* (an evil water-sprite), *sonsie* (prosperous or comfortable, or, by a later semantic development, plump), *ingle* (domestic fire or hearth), *caird* (tinker), *clachan* (village, or alehouse), *tocher* (dowry), *caur* (left, as in *caurie-clookit,* left-handed), *clavers* (chat), *brat* (rag, or apron), *crummock* (crooked stick), *mant* (stammer), and some terms relating to the preparation of food such as *sowens* (a paste-like preparation from oat-husks), *drammock* (oatmeal stirred in water), *bladdoch* (buttermilk) and *brochan* (gruel). These have been common currency in Scots for a long time: more recent Gaelic borrowings generally refer to features of Highland culture and date from the emergence of a romantic interest in the now safely disarmed Highlands on the part of the Lowlanders: *claymore* (literally "big sword"), *skean dhu* (literally "black knife"), *caber, sporran, clarsach, brogue* (shoe), *clan, coronach, philibeg.* The fact that some of these words have now become generally known outside Scotland, and form part of the popular tourist image of Scotland and its inhabitants, is largely owing to Sir Walter Scott; and their prevalence in his novels is indicative of a change in the relative status of the two cultures of Scotland. The Highlands were now defeated, disarmed and reduced to political and military impotence; and therefore their traditional way of life could become the object of a popular romantic interest, resulting in the widespread diffusion of a colourful and exciting "image" only tenuously related to the facts of Highland history.[32] (This situation is by no means unique: compare, for example, the contrast between the actual history of the aboriginal North Americans and the "Red Indians" of popular mythology.)

Another important contributor to the Scots language was French. English too, as is well known, has adopted vast numbers of French words: the Anglo-Saxon tongues of both countries, in fact, were sub-

jected to pervasive French influence in the period following the
Norman conquest of England and what is often called the "peaceful
Norman conquest" of Scotland. However, the history and the effects
of French in the two countries differ somewhat. In England the
accession of William the Conqueror resulted in the temporary
eclipse of the entire tradition of government through the Anglo-
Saxon tongue. Not only was the Saxon royal line dispossessed but
all its governmental institutions were replaced by the Norman feudal system, established throughout the kingdom by French legisla-
tors and administrators. The governing class was entirely French in
language and culture, and French scribes carried the King's writ to
all parts of his domain. The kings themselves, for several generations, were not only French speakers but Frenchmen: even two hundred years after the Conquest, Edward Langshanks (1272–1307),
though his reign certainly marked a reaction from that of the whole-
heartedly Francophile Henry III (1216–72), was in himself scarcely
more of an Englishman than Richard Coeur de Lion (1184–99) had
been.

It was not until the middle of the fourteenth century that English
began to replace French in the law courts, and not until the end of
it that a king (Henry IV) took his coronation oath in English. In
Scotland, though the last monarchs of the Celtic line adopted
French as their court language, they were and remained native-born
Scots: French had nothing like the social importance that it had in
England; nor – since Scotland lacked the massive bureaucracy of
Norman and Plantagenet England – did it ever become an integral
part of the machinery of government. French linguistic influence
in Scotland was therefore more voluntary, so to speak, than in the
neighbouring kingdom. It was also longer lasting. Anglo-French
hostility and Scoto-French alliance were almost invariable features
of European politics throughout the Middle Ages and beyond; and
the close relationship between Scotland and France, and consequent
familiarity of the Scots nobility with things French, led to a more
intimate and durable penetration of the national language and culture by those of Scotland's partner in the Auld Alliance. The contrasting relations of Scotland and England with the leading cultural
power in Western Europe do not provide a full explanation, but it is
hard not to see them as a contributory factor, to the excellence of
Scottish and the poverty of English literature during most of the

fifteenth century.

The language of Barbour's *Brus* shows French influence of a practical kind: an abundance of interesting military terms.[33] Several still-recognisable words have their first Scottish, or first ever, attestation in this text: *assaile, baner, campioun* (the Norman form of *champion*), *fortrass* and *harnes.* So too have some now known only to mediaeval scholars: *arsoun* (saddle-bow), *assenye* (war-cry), *eschell* (battalion), *quyrbolle* (*cuir bouillé*, pressed and moulded leather, used as material for armour), *tropell* (troop) and *vyre* (crossbow bolt). *Merdale*, which in Barbour means camp followers, survives in some dialects to the present day, despite its unpleasing derivation, in the sense of a crowd.

In Barbour, characteristically, the French contribution is useful rather than ornamental. Later, the increasing elaboration of literary Scots led to a growth in French influence of a more decorative kind. The most extreme example is probably the anonymous *Complaint of Scotland*, an impassioned denunciation of English aggression and appeal for a strengthening of the Auld Alliance as a means of preserving the Scottish national identity and integrity. The *Complaint* is dedicated to Mary of Guise, Queen Regent since the death of her husband James V and the chief hope of the pro-French party in Scotland; and appropriately its language abounds in such terms as *afflige, dedie, gazophile, salutiffere* and *temerare,* besides giving *amplitude, machine* and other now-familiar Gallicisms to the common word-stock.

The contribution of French to the Scots vocabulary is far from being restricted to the mediaeval period: many familiar and characteristic Scots words are from this source. Some are instantly recognisable to anyone with even an elementary knowledge of French: *ashet, bien, braw* (from *brave*), *douce, dour, fash, gigot, tass.* Others require a more intimate acquaintance with both languages for the relationship to be apparent: *aippleringie* (southernwood, a fragrant shrub), *arles* (fee paid in advance), *bawsint* (having a white stripe down the face like Burns's Luath), *bigget* (a linen cap), *cummer* (female friend or gossip), *dams* (game of draughts), *disjune* (breakfast), *gean* (wild cherry), *grosset* (gooseberry), *houlet* (owl), *ladron* (rascal), *plenishins* (furniture), *turcas* (pliers), *bonnallay* (a farewell drink, from *bon aller*), *Hogmanay* (from *aguillaneuf*, a New Year's gift), and the warning call, no longer to be heard daily in the streets of Edinburgh but still surviving in popular lore, *gardyloo* (from *garde à l'eau*).

Scotland's connection with France has always appealed to the imagination because of the colourful personages and events with which it is associated. Less spectacular, but at least equally important as a cultural influence, was a trading partnership with the Netherlands which, like the Auld Alliance, remained constant throughout the Middle Ages. Flemings were arriving in Scotland as settlers as early as the twelfth century, their skill in weaving and other crafts making them valuable immigrants; merchants of Scotland and the Netherlands had reciprocal privileges in each other's country; and unlike the Auld Alliance the Dutch connection was not terminated but strengthened by the Reformation, when both countries adopted the Calvinist form of Protestantism. The homely nature of many Dutch borrowings bears witness to the easy familiarity which must have characterised Scoto-Dutch interaction and the pervasive influence – not, of course, all one-sided – of one culture on the other.[34] We have *craig* (neck), *cuit* (ankle) and *dowp* (backside), farming terms such as *bucht* (sheep pen), *farrow* (a cow when not in calf), *heck* or *haik* (a hay rack), *cavie* (a hen coop), *kesart* (cheese vat), *owsen* (oxen), and terms relating to commonplace features of everyday life: *callant* (fellow), *doit* (small coin), *geck* (scornful gesture), *howff* (inn), *mutch* (lady's bonnet), *mutchkin* (a measure of capacity), *redd* (tidy up), *track-pot* (teapot): even *scone* is Dutch.

One more major foreign influence on Scots is that of the Scandinavian tongues. In the dialects of the Northern Isles and Caithness, Scandinavian words abound for a particular reason: these areas were among those settled by Vikings in the ninth and tenth centuries; and long after they reverted to Scottish rule – the northern mainland in the reign of William the Lion, the Isles as late as that of James III – Norse continued there as a spoken tongue, surviving in Orkney until the eighteenth century and in Shetland, at least in fragmentary form, even until the nineteenth. The northernmost dialects of Scots therefore contain numerous Scandinavian-derived words not found elsewhere. (For the same reason, the dialects of areas such as Kintyre, Galloway and Morayshire, where Gaelic was spoken until recently, contain far more Gaelic borrowings than those of Central and Southern Scotland.) As a few examples of Norse influence, we may cite (from Caithness) *aikle* (molar tooth), *clinkertonie* (jellyfish), *marfloo* (sea louse), and *tuskar* (spade for cutting peat); from Orkney *alamotti* (storm petrel), *arro* (chickweed), *brooser* (red face), *muggro-fue* (drizzling mist), *reevligo* (rash, excitable), and *vandit* (striped, of cattle); and from Shetland, which outshines the other two areas in the wealth of Norse-derived words still surviving in its vocabulary, *blogga* (marsh marigold), *cockalorie* (daisy), *smora* (clover), *lorin* (cormorant), *swaabie* (great black-backed gull), *shalder* (oyster-catcher), *aandoo* (row against the tide to keep the boat stationary), *brimtud* (sound of waves crashing on the shore), *mareel* (phosphorescent plankton), *roost* (strong tidal current), *shürmal* (foreshore), *vaddle* (tidal pool).

The "mainstream" dialects of Scots also show considerable Norse influence, but it came by a somewhat different route. Viking settlements in England had resulted by the late ninth century in a virtual Norse-speaking territory, formally recognised by Alfred the Great; and though Saxon rule over the Danish-held areas was gradually recovered by Alfred's successors, this did not result in the expulsion of all Norse-speakers, nor of their cultural and linguistic influence. This influence was further strengthened when Sweyn Forkbeard and Cnut subjected most of England once again to Danish rule. All forms of Anglo-Saxon spoken in England were greatly affected by Scandinavian; but in the Danelaw this influence was so fundamental as to produce almost a hybrid of the two closely-related languages, Anglo-Saxon and Norse. The English refugees and other settlers who, as we have seen, swelled the population of Anglo-Saxon-speaking Scotland in the later eleventh and twelfth centuries brought this Anglo-Norse dialect with them: to this day, Northern English dialects contain many Norse words whose domains straddle the Anglo-Scottish border. The Norse contributions to the Scots vocabulary includes words more basic than even Dutch has given: *gar* (make), *maun* (must), *tyne* (lose), *big* (build), *hing* (hang), *lass* (girl), *harns* (brains), *hause* (neck), *neive* (fist), *luif* (palm), *lug* (ear), *brae* (hill), *gowk* (cuckoo), *lowe* (flame), *lowse* (finish work), *nowt* (cattle), *lowp* (jump), *meikle* (big) – and even *kilt*.

What this abundant, varied and productive foreign influence should show is that Scots was once the language of a cosmopolitan, adventurous, outward-looking people, whose country, small and isolated though it was, played a full part in the economic, political and artistic life of Europe. Scotland did not maintain this status; and the tongue declined with the nation. And though those of us who today advocate a greater degree of support for Scots may blame our predecessors for their failure to preserve the integrity of the language, we must acknowledge that their motives were comprehensible. In the passions aroused by the Reformation controversies, the fate of the language was not seen as a matter of great moment, particularly since even the practice of regarding Scots as a distinct language from English was relatively new and not universally followed: Catholic spokesmen sometimes used their antagonists' preference for the English language as a debating point,[35] but to John Knox, who had preached for several years in England and among English exiles in Frankfurt and Geneva, the opening of Scotland to English influence would have seemed a small price to pay for the establishment of Protestantism in Scotland – if he gave consideration to the matter at all. James VI, a man of cosmopolitan outlook in literature as well as in politics, tried deliberately to restore French and Italian culture to their position of influence on Scottish life and letters, but the ancient links could not be fully recovered; and even before 1603 many Scotsmen in high positions were acquiring English in anticipation of the King's eventual accession to the English throne. English, even in the late sixteenth century, was thus coming to be seen in Scotland as a passport to social and economic advancement.

As Scotland progressively lost its status as an independent nation, its language was first assimilated to English and then replaced by it in one field of usage after another, leading eventually to the present virtual restriction of Scots to domestic conversation and literature. But if Scotland is not for the present able to participate on its own terms in free and mutually enriching cultural interaction with sovereign nations, we at least have in our language a memorial to the time when we were – if we care to preserve even that.

It is not to be imagined that when the influence of foreign languages on Scots declined, the tongue ceased altogether to develop: on the contrary, in its more restricted spheres it found new resources from within itself, and its subsequent history is no less revealing of its social and cultural setting. No longer the language of the aristocracy, it remained that of the peasants; and the distinctive speech of the rural communities continued in vigorous life. Robert Burns, the archetypal voice of his class, showed – not only in his poems, but in the fascinating definitions and notes which he provided in his glossaries – how precisely the language was geared to the minutiae of country life: examples such as *stimpart* (literally "sixteenth part", a measure of grain), *thrave* (two stooks of twelve sheaves), *fittie-lan* (glossed by Burns as "the near horse of the hindmost pair in the plough"), *risk* ("to make a noise like the breaking of small roots with the plough"), *knappin-hammer* ("a hammer for breaking stones"), *broose* ("a race at country weddings who shall first reach the bridegroom's house on returning from church"), *flingin-tree* ("a piece of timber hung by way of partition between two horses in a stable, a flail") can be found in abundance.

As the age of improvement progressed in Scotland and agriculture changed from subsistence to commercial farming, a whole range of specialised technical vocabulary arose: this perhaps reached its greatest richness in the North-East with its distinctive system of large-scale arable farming. Burns mentions *pattle* and *coulter* (shaft and blade of a plough); but later we find reference to *socks, skreefers, soams, theets, muzzles, sheckles, sheths* and *treadwiddies* as specific parts of a plough or plough harness. It is perhaps an indication of the extent to which farming methods were seen to have improved in the nineteenth century that an old-fashioned type of plough with no separate coulter came to be nicknamed a *Robbie Burns*!

Other industries as practised in Scotland acquired their distinctive terminology, maintaining the language in a state of healthy development. Fishing boats such as *Fifies, nabbies, baldies, yoles* and *Zulus* were equipped with nets which would be weighted with *lug-stanes* and suspended by *noozles* from the *heid-bauk*; or with lines to the *snuids* of which the hooks were attached by *tippins*. Coal miners in pits propped with *stells* or *rances* used *hawks* to extract *cherry coal, parrot coal, splint coal* or merely *humph*, and loaded it into *hutches*. A special case is the ancient and venerable edifice of Scots law, of which the distinctive terminology, abounding in words from Latin and French, is an exception to the general decline of foreign influence on Scots. *Exeem* (exempt), *depone* (declare upon oath), *delate* (accuse before a court), *demit* (resign), *adduce* (produce as proof), *forfaulture* (forfeiture), *avisandum* (further consideration): these and many more legal expressions, some surviving from earlier periods and others being adopted during the Enlightenment, show that the continuing vitality of Scots was not solely the responsibility of the

peasant and artisan classes. (This somewhat idiosyncratic feature of
the language, the unusual preponderance of distinctive legal terms,
bears witness to the socio-historical fact that large numbers of ambi-
tious young men in eighteenth-century Scotland studied law as a
means of advancement, and proportionately far more than now
among the country's intelligentsia were lawyers by training.)

Burns's contribution to the language did not consist only in the literary exploitation of the vocabulary of rural life. He also demonstrated the virtually untapped wealth of the language's popular register: many words thitherto rarely used in literature, sometimes for
the simple reason that their referents are not such as normally con-
cern poets, appeared in his work and (in some cases) thereafter
became common literary currency. *Histie* (dry, barren), *icker* (ear of
corn), *tawie* (docile, tractable), *winze* (oath) and *ier-oe* (great grand-
child) have few attestations before Burns; *forjeskit* (tired), *grushie*
("of thick, stout growth"), *snash* (abusive language) and *outler*
("lying in the fields, not housed at night") have virtually none, or
none between his time and the Middle Ages; *ramfeezled* (exhausted),
splore ("a frolic, a riot, a noise"), *hog-shouther* (jostle) and *penny-
wheep* (small beer) appear to be his own concoctions.

In the present century, two major historical changes have left their
marks on the language. One is the transition in Scotland from a rural
agricultural to an urban industrial society. This has had the
inevitable effect that large numbers of words associated with farming life – a huge area of the traditional Scots vocabulary – have virtually or completely disappeared from active use. On the other
hand, the vigorous and highly distinctive urban patois which has
arisen, besides being used (as already noted) for literary effect, has
added a new dimension to the spoken language. One would search
in vain in the SND or earlier reference works for *bowfin* (stinking),
marock (drunk), *stoater* (a "smasher"), *monty* (hurry up), *geggie*
(mouth), *jeggie* (any fizzy drink), *heidbanger* (lunatic), *heidnipper*
(termagant); but these and other memorable expressions regularly
enliven conversations in city pubs and playgrounds. The other is
the re-appropriation of Scots by literati with a scholarly bent. The
practice of developing the language by unearthing its buried trea-
sures was known, as we have just seen, even in Burns's time; but the
Scots of the great modern poets discussed in the previous chapter
contains not only words taken directly from the mediaeval language,

but words concocted on the model of mediaeval usages – a still more interesting practice, since it shows the learned register of the language still to be living and productive. No Scots poet of the Stewart period used the words *ayebidan, dumfounrous, conturbatioun* or *orsplendant*, but Douglas Young or Sidney Goodsir Smith, at their best, can persuade us that the language and the register in which such words once appeared is still sufficiently alive for those and others to be created, as Dunbar could have created them if he had required.

In these ways, the history of the Scots language reflects the history of the Scots-speaking community. Neither, despite long-standing pressures and gloomy predictions, has as yet become a topic of purely historical interest: there is no need that they ever should.

Five
Why it matters:
as a means of communication

Scots is the way many people speak (a fact which tends to be overlooked); and the most cursory glance at the Scots word-stock, and at the speech habits of Scotsmen as recorded through the centuries and as still heard today, will reveal an idiom with a unique and unmistakable character. Whether the Scots populace has an innate skill in verbal inventiveness, or whether the nature of the language is such as to inspire its speakers to unusual fluency and wit, is an academic question: the certain fact is that not only in literature but in ordinary speech Scots is an expressive medium of remarkable potential. Even today, when the number of people having a full command of the traditional vocabulary is relatively small and diminishing, the verbal resourcefulness of some Scots speakers is a matter of ready observation; and it is noteworthy that the recently-developed urban dialects, despised though they are in some quarters, show every bit as much creative life as the more respected rural speech forms.

Even a casual acquaintance with the language and its literature will reveal words with distinctive semantic resonances. "Now they're crouse and canty baith":[36] what is the English equivalent for that line? Burns himself, in the glossary to the 1787 edition of his poems, explained *crouse* as "chearful, courageous" and *cantie* as "chearful, merry". But "Now they're both cheerful and merry" does not begin to convey the precise sense of comfortable, companionable domesticity suggested by the Scots. "Ablachs and scrats and dorbels o' a' kinds":[37] Scots has always afforded unlimited scope for insults, from the period when Dunbar could address a rival poet with

> Mauch muttoun, bit buttoun, peilit gluttoun, air to Hilhous;
> Rank beggar, ostir dregar, foule flegar in the flet ....[38]

to the era when a character in a play by Roddy MacMillan could blister another with "Ya knee-crept, Jesus-crept, swatchin little fucker ... ya hure-spun, bastrified, conscrapulated young prick"[39]; and MacDiarmid could have chosen those three particular terms from

49

among dozens: *bam, baigle, bauchle, bizzum, blastie, blellum, blether-skite, daw, dobbie, duddron, dreep, gomeral, glumph, haverall, limmer, jaud, nabal, nyaff, nickum, scrog, scrunt, skypel, shilp, smeowt, sumph, skellum, tawpie, tumphie, tink, tyke, wurf* and *wallidrag,* for instance. But each of those words has its own field of reference, and MacDiarmid has selected three which convey the exact mixture of repugnance and contempt appropriate to his purpose. This is hardly the most serious argument in favour of a revival of Scots; but what a loss it would be if, as appears to be very nearly the case, we forgot all those expressive and accurate insult terms and were reduced to the two or three all-purpose obscenities used with such pathetic monotony in many people's speech today![40]

Naturally, Scots has many words with nothing especially remarkable or interesting about them: a soutar is nothing more nor less than a cobbler, a teuchat than a lapwing, a brace than a mantelpiece, a neive than a fist. But it is undeniable that Scots exploits the possibilities of phonaesthetic expression (i.e. the emotive power of the actual *sounds* of the word) to an extent that has no parallel in Western European languages. To begin with the most extreme examples, consider the fanciful polysyllabic coinages which have always been such a striking feature of Scots. As a randomly-chosen dozen, we may cite *cattiewurrie* (a noisy dispute), *clamihewit* (a heavy blow), *curryborum* (a noisy crowd in a small space), *eerie-orums* (details, especially of a finicky sort), *flichtmafletheries* (useless or excessive ornamentation), *fliskmahaigo* (a frivolous woman), *hal-larackit* (harebrained, boisterous), *heeligoleerie* (in a confused state), *heelstergowdie* (head over heels), *malagrugrous* (dismal, forbidding), *ramageichan* (an awkward or simple person), and *tappietourie* (a pile or peak). To dismiss these and the many comparable forms that exist as merely amusing would be a superficial reaction; though of course some are deliberately comical. In themselves and in their abundance they demonstrate an exuberant fondness on the part of Scots speakers for playing with the expressive force of sounds. Some have recognisable etymologies: *cattiewurrie* is from the Dutch *kater* (tom cat) combined with *wurr* (a dog's growl), and *tappietourie* unites *tap* and *tour* (tower); others are simply concoctions bearing little relationship to any previously existing form: all, however, are certainly memorable words. The fact that few of them are attested with any degree of frequency is significant: in the context in which they were first used they were probably off-the-cuff inventions, yet the speakers or writers could produce them in confidence that they would be accepted as *meaningful*, not as mere gibberish: they were produced, that is, within a strongly-developed tradition of verbal creativity. (Is it conceivable that this characteristic of Scots has its origin in the many lengthy and highly distinctive place-names, incomprehensible to Lowlanders though often possessing a perfectly straightforward Gaelic etymology, which dot the toponymic map of Scotland – Auchterarder, Auchenfedrick, Barmuckity, Balmaclellan, Ecclefechan, Maggieknockater? The regular recurrence of the syllable -*ma*-, meaningless in itself, in those long words suggests an influence from Gaelic-derived names.)

It is not only in these really extravagant forms that the peculiar expressive force of Scots is demonstrated: words which are less arresting at first glance, but which nonetheless stick in the mind because of a distinctive semantic implication, sound pattern, or both, exist in hundreds. To discuss individually even the beginning of a representative selection would clearly be impossible: for the uninitiated, the best way to make their acquaintance is to read the literature, or to spend a leisure hour browsing in the pages of the *Scottish National Dictionary*. (From there one may graduate to conversing with a native speaker.) But consider what it must be to ficher, footer, plitter, scutter, sotter and taver, or to daidle, haingle, hushle, taigle, wammle and wauchle; to feel disjaskit or forfochen, bambaizit or jurmummelt, wabbit or trauchelt, dwaiblie or dowff; to find yourself in a fasherie, fykerie, carfuffle or slaister; to be scunnert or stamagastert by something ugsome, fousome, mauchie or ramsh; to participate in a splore, a stramash or a gilravage; to suffer a clour, a dirl, a skelp, a sklaff, a dirdum, a dunshach or a lounder; to be made to glunch or grue, to snirt or snicher, to wheenge or peenge; to play a gunk or a geck, a plunkie, pliskie or prattiken; to find one acquaintance thowless, fusionless, doitit and donnert, another grippy, grabby, nippit and moulie, a third gleg, trig, perjink and jinniperous, and a fourth blye, douce, leesome and leal; to be out in the blowts and blufferts of a gowsterous gale or the smochy smore of a rouky mist – and having considered, Anglophone reader, tell me that you still find Scots incomprehensible! This most onomatopoeic of languages speaks for itself in accents that can appeal to the ear of anybody not suffering from the self-inflicted deafness of prejudice. The linguistic inventiveness of many twentieth-century poets has yielded impressive results, but the fact that they have shown such inventiveness is itself not remarkable: what is surprising is that a language with such resources should ever have sunk into a period of creative barrenness which it required the energy of a MacDiarmid to dispel.

This wealth of emotive words is not the only idiosyncratic feature of Scots. Another is a fondness for compound words in which a mental or moral characteristic is expressed in a (literal or fanciful) physical description. Thus *heich-heidit* is vain or arrogant, *lang-heidit* shrewd or sagacious, *lang-luggit* inquisitive, *flea-luggit* eccentric or whimsical, *hingin-luggit* dejected, *nerra-nebbit* bigoted, *lang-lippit* sulky, *souple-neckit* obsequious, *glib-gabbit* voluble, *fou-haunit* wealthy, *fou-breekit* pompous, *parritch-hertit* sentimental. Another is a tendency to metaphorical expression: *to hae aa yer back teeth* is to be wise and watchful for possible deceptions, *to pit a body's gas at a peep* is to show him up in an unimpressive light, *to ding doon Tantallon* is to attempt the impossible, *to be like a knotless threid* is to behave in an aimless, helpless manner, *to tak a guid grip o Scotland* is to have big feet, *to gar a body's een staun in backwater* is to reduce him to helplessness, *to get yer kail throu the reek* is to suffer a severe scolding, *to kaim against the hair* is to irritate or tease, *to gae roun the mou wi an English dishclout* is to become affectedly Anglicised in speech, *to ride the riggin o the Kirk* is to be excessively partisan. A fat person is *as ready to rowe as rin*, a mean person *wad rake Hell for a bodle*, a talkative person *has a tongue that wad clip clouts*, a person who is smarter than he appears is *no as green as he's cabbage-luikin*. Still another feature of our language, closely related to the last, is a fondness for proverbial or aphoristic expressions: collections of these, of which there have been many since the eighteenth century, may include well over a thousand items; and this habit of Scots speakers is easily recognizable both in literature (many of Walter Scott's characters, for instance, are walking treasuries of proverbial wisdom) and in everyday speech. Once again, first-hand observation of the language itself, in both its written and its spoken forms, is the best way to become acquainted with this aspect of it; but, as a tiny sampling, we may cite the following: "It's ill bringing but whit's no there ben" – "He that mairries or [before] he be wise will

die or he be rich" – "A dog winna youl gin ye strike him wi a bane"
– "Better a wee bush than nae bield" – "He that's far frae his gear is
near tae his tinsel" – "There was never a guid toun but there was a
dub at the end o't" – "We aa come tae the ae door at nicht" – "Ilka
cock craws crouse on his ain midden heid" – "Naething's gotten
athout pains but dirt and lang nails" – "The soutar's wife's aye the
warst shod" – "For faut o wise fowk fuils sit on binks" – "Fair fowk
are aye fusionless". If the cornucopia of fanciful words that we have
noted show the tendency of the Scots to flights of the imagination,
the proverbs show another side to the national character: shrewd,
cautious, hard-headed, patient, and without illusions regarding life
and humanity.[41]

It is perhaps surprising that the way of life from which these
proverbs emerged, to the narrow and wearisome nature of which
they bear ready witness, should have produced such a verbal and
voluble people, but the fact remains; and in the equally uninspiring
surroundings of modern city tenements and slums, the wit of the
Scots continues to flourish undaunted. Schoolteachers who despair
of eliciting any response from children in the assertively "proper-
English"-speaking environment of classrooms have been known to
be surprised at the fluency of their charges when they resume their
native vernacular in the playgound.

This last point is an illustration on one level of the harm that has
been done to the national self-confidence, as well as to the Scots language itself, by the traditional enforcement of English and suppres-
sion of Scots in the schools. One wonders if the teachers who have
dutifully perpetrated this iniquity through the generations have
ever taken a close look at what they are trying to destroy.

The discussion of Scots as a means of communication may be con-
cluded on a speculative note. The Scots tongue, with its wealth of
striking and memorable words and expressions, could if allowed to
reclaim its place have far-reaching effects on the intellectual life of
not only Scotland but the world. English, as is well known, has
acceded to a position of universal dominance unapproached by any
other language in history, and unlikely to be challenged in the fore-
seeable future. This is due in part to the enormous social and economic importance of Great Britain in the nineteenth and early twentieth centuries and of the United States in the later twentieth; but it
is also due to the fact (as it certainly is) that English is easier to

learn, at least at a basic level, than many other languages. But as the
possession of a basic knowledge of English becomes more neces-
sary, and more widespread, throughout the world, native speakers of
the language are now in danger of themselves becoming content
with a basic knowledge: it has often been observed that in the
principal English-speaking countries the language, in its spoken and
written forms, is increasingly limited to its simplest, least imaginative and least challenging registers.[42] Its utilitarian use as a language
of technology, commerce, tourism and mass entertainment has
undermined its status as a vehicle for work of literary and intellectual distinction; and the sheer quantity of dross produced in the language makes it progressively more difficult for works of merit to
receive widespread attention. The language which enjoys one of the
greatest – arguably the very greatest – among the world's treasury of
national literatures is in real danger of cultural degeneracy. The
rediscovery of the full resources of Scots by MacDiarmid and his
successors gave to Scottish writing a shot in the arm of which the
effects show no signs of being spent. If Scotland's populace as a
whole, instead of only her literati and scholars, made a vigorous
effort to promote their language, and thus attracted the attention of
educated readers and writers in other countries, could the vitality of
Scots exert a beneficial influence on the entire English-speaking
world?

Six
And another reason

THE ARGUMENT OF THE PREVIOUS three chapters has been that Scots matters because it is inherently valuable: not only to the Scottish populace, be it noted, but to the world, as embodying the contribution made by one of the world's nations to the totality of human achievement. But there is another aspect to the issue. The Scots language is a mark of the distinctive identity of the Scottish people; and as such we should be concerned to preserve it, even if there were no other reason, because it is *ours*. This statement requires neither explanation nor apology. A full discussion of the concept of nationhood would be far beyond the scope of this book; but it is incontestable that a sense of national identity entails the sense of being distinct from other nations. To be Portuguese means, among many other things, not to be Spanish. It is easy to denigrate this attitude on the grounds that it may, and often does, give rise to mutual suspicion and hostility; but it is to the differences between national cultures that we owe the glorious diversity of human artistic and intellectual endeavour. To imagine that one's own nation is inherently superior to another is folly at best, but there is neither sin nor shame in feeling, and showing, pride in what is both distinctive and admirable in one's native culture. And in our own days, when the technology of mass communication is threatening to submerge all but the largest – which does not necessarily mean the finest – of cultures in a uniformity of the trivial and banal, it is more important than ever to the continuing vitality of the human intellect that the distinctiveness of small national cultures should be maintained. There is no contradiction between this and the need, which requires no emphasis, for mutual understanding and tolerance between peoples. The desideratum for mankind is not a cultural uniformity with all regional and national differences of religion, language, aesthetics, moral and philosophical attitudes and material civilisation merged in a single unvarying pattern, but a world in which the multifarious cultures flourish independently, each learning from the others and freely interchanging influences as needed and desired, in a vital and vibrant creative diversity. To be Portuguese is not to be Spanish, and to be Scottish is not to be English: when these statements can be made freely, with neither Portuguese nor Spaniard, neither Scot nor Englishman, seeing in them either an implied gibe or an implied threat, mankind will have made real and fundamental progress.

The statement that the Scots tongue is a mark of Scottish nationality must not be taken as meaning more than it says. Scots is not, of course, the *only* linguistic mark of Scottish nationality; nor is Scottish nationality a possession only of those who speak Scots. Gaelic and English too are languages of Scotland. The last-named is an international language in which the English have no longer any proprietary rights: it belongs to us equally with them, and with the Americans, Canadians, Australians and many other peoples. But although we have developed it in distinctive ways – Scottish-accented English is at once recognisable, and many Scottish writers using English as their medium have found it no handicap in expressing their Scottish identity – it is not *uniquely* ours. Scots, by contrast, is a language spoken nowhere else in the world. Obvious though it seems, this is not unworthy of remark. Several dialects of German, originating in the homeland, have been preserved by immigrants in the New World: Pennsylvania Dutch (a form of German, despite its misleading English name), and the dialects of the Mennonite and Hutterite communities are outstanding examples, and small colonies of German speakers in South America and Australasia have preserved dialectal forms. This situation is quite distinct from the emergence of a new dialect *after* colonial settlement, such as the "Cajun" French of New Orleans.[43] But despite the vast number of Scots who have emigrated in the last two centuries, there appears to be no clear case of Scots surviving outwith Scotland as a community language, as Gaelic survived until recently in Argentina and has endured to the present day, in some cases through an astonishing seven generations, in Nova Scotia:[44] all that remains of a Scots linguistic presence overseas is a handful of dialect words in the folk-speech of some regions of eastern North America and New Zealand.[45] There is even a sense in which Scots is a more purely Scottish language than Gaelic, though the Gaelic tongue was established in what is now Scotland before the Anglo-Saxon: Scots was recognisably distinct from English, even Northern English, by the end of the fourteenth century, whereas we have no evidence that the

Scottish and Irish varieties of Gaelic, at least in their written forms (it is impossible to trace the history of the spoken forms with certainty) had diverged significantly before the sixteenth.

Very often, an intimate association is found to exist between a nation and its language. The Polish tongue was one of the things that preserved a national community in being during the period when no Polish state existed; the German-speaking people possessed a strong national identity before the political union of Germany; Finnish, Czech and Slovak are examples of languages preserved as a unifying force among their speakers when oppressed by a foreign culture. It is not the case that a nation *needs* a language unique and proper to itself in order to exist as a nation: the Spanish-speaking countries of the Americas all show a strong sense of individual nationalism and some have developed highly distinctive national cultures: but instances can readily be found of countries placing particular emphasis on some linguistic idiosyncrasy for nationalistic reasons. Romansch, though by far the least considerable both culturally and demographically of the four languages of Switzerland, has officially equal status with the others because it is the only language peculiar to the country; in Peru, where unlike Mexico little regard is paid to the imposing heritage of the pre-Conquest civilizations, the recent elevation of the indigenous language Quechua to official status was also an act of linguistic nationalism. In the Scots tongue, Scotland has a national symbol of enormous potential. It cannot be realistically envisaged that Scots (or Gaelic for that matter) could displace English entirely from a position of importance in the national life; but there can be no doubt that the distinctiveness of Scotland in the eyes of the rest of the world would be enhanced if the Scots language were assigned a more conspicuous place. The cultural and historical importance of the language speaks for itself. The population of Scotland should speak for the language too, simply because it is a distinctive national possession.

Seven
What should we do?

T HE SCOTS LANGUAGE IS A priceless national treasure. That is no overstatement nor expression of romantic partisanship: a tongue which has been the vehicle of some of Europe's outstanding literary works, which in its wealth of colourful vocabulary and idiom lends itself to such striking colloquial and literary expression, and which conveys as no other can the fiery imagination, incisive intellect, tough stoicism and gentle affection that are aspects of the Scottish character is certainly nothing less. Yet because of a disastrous capitulation to alien values, we have treated this national treasure as a thing of no moment: have allowed it to deteriorate in status and in scope, to occupy an ever-diminishing place in the national life, and in our own time to come under the threat of actual extinction. No one who is familiar with even a part of the corpus of Scots literature, no one with an interest in language and its resources, least of all anyone who believes that the native institutions of a people – the things which give that people its distinctive identity – are worth preserving for that reason alone, can contemplate the decline of Scots unmoved.

The situation is of course not unique. Languages and dialects have disappeared and are now disappearing elsewhere in the world: the process is, and perhaps always has been, a regularly recurring feature of human interaction.[46] Sometimes – more frequently than is generally realised, especially in the present day – the disappearance of a language may be due to plain genocide: in Australasia and the Americas, for example, there is no telling how many languages and cultures have been lost with the deliberate extermination of native peoples during the centuries of white expansion; and let no one imagine that the process is at an end. In other cases, languages have been abandoned by their speakers for what are perceived as culturally or materially more desirable speech forms. Often such a language shift is made under overt political or social pressure, backed up in some cases by physical force, from the dominant power: imperialist government languages such as Latin, Russian and

English have submerged many other tongues in their geopolitical spheres of influence; and one of the most remarkable instances from further afield is Quechua, transformed in a mere century from the local speech of an unimportant tribe to the all-conquering tongue of the magnificent Inca Empire. English today poses a more deadly threat to other languages than any tongue has presented before: established on every continent during the colonial and imperial centuries, and now supported not only by the overwhelming economic power of the United States but, more deplorably, by the low-quality entertainment broadcast daily to all corners of the world, it has actually been seen by some scholars as threatening even the smaller European national languages, such as those of the Scandinavian states, with extinction in their own homelands.[47]

But if the death of a language is a common event, that does not make it a desirable one; and the speakers of threatened languages have in some cases shown themselves able to withstand the threat and preserve their tongue as a living speech. Danish, Finnish, Czech and Slovak, Icelandic, Faroese and Letzeburgesch are examples of speech forms which in this or the last century have emerged from a disadvantaged position to become established national languages; at present, Alsatian and Swiss German are among the threatened languages which are at any rate vigorously supported by a conscious local patriotism. For Scots, the position is not beyond hope. The first and most urgent necessity, however, is to disencumber ourselves of the attitude which has crippled the national life for generations: the notion that what is English is natural and right, and what is Scottish a provincial aberration. It was the astonishing "failure of intellectual nerve"[48] that afflicted Scotland in the early nineteenth century which led to this assumption. A widespread feature of the splendid period of intellectual achievement known as the Enlightenment had been a determined attempt by the Scottish intelligentsia to abandon their speech for English: an attitude which can be readily enough explained by the sense which they had of belonging to a new era in which the unhappy past and everything associated with it could be forgotten. David Hume had his works carefully checked for Scots expressions and compiled a list of Scottish words and idioms to avoid; other scholars too made lists of "Scotticisms" – "to put young writers and speakers on their guard against some of those Scotch idioms which in this country are liable to be mistaken for English".[49] But notwithstanding their hostility to the Scots tongue, Hume and his contemporaries had no intention of making themselves into Englishmen. In the nineteenth century, however, even the name and identity of Scotland, and everything that made it distinctively Scottish, became suspect, as the Scots came to regard English mores as the English themselves regarded them – as the natural models for the rest of the world. Occasional manifestations of cultural nationalism there were, but on the whole an Anglocentric habit of mind became prevalent. It is, indeed, very odd that those who have shown themselves most anxious to avoid "provincialism" or "insularity" by divesting themselves of Scottish characteristics should have failed to see that there is no surer sign of a provincial mentality than to accept unquestioningly the attitudes of one particular society, including that society's attitudes to one's own, as if they were part of the natural order of things. To the extent that Scots is a provincial dialect, it became so when Scotland began to think of itself as a province instead of a nation. The attitude of the Scottish people that their native language is something to be ashamed of – or at best, something for which a nostalgia-shrouded niche may be preserved in the English-speaking society – parallels that of natives in colonialised territories under the rule of an imperial government: it is not a becoming standpoint for a people with claims to nationhood.

There are unmistakable signs that this attitude is at last being put aside. A major boost to the status of Scots has been its recent recognition by the European Bureau of Lesser-Used Languages. This body is actively seeking information on Scots to add to its hitherto sparse files on the language, and its pamphlet *Scotland: a Linguistic Double Helix* (by Iseabail Macleod and Aonghas Mac Neacaill),[50] one of an ongoing series of booklets on the smaller European languages, discusses Gaelic and Scots on an equal footing. It would indeed be a disgrace if we ourselves, now that our language has been granted this expression of confidence by the European Community, failed to demonstrate our own belief in its value.

At the time of writing, efforts are in train to have a question on Scots included in the next Census. This, if successful, would be an important gain for several reasons. First, it would provide at least some information on the number of Scots-speakers, the areas where

the language has its strongest power-bases, and the extent to which
its use can be associated with factors such as age, sex and class: the
availability from census returns of such information on Gaelic has
been of great value in devising social and educational policies for
that language. Information so obtained on Scots would probably be
much less certain than that on Gaelic, since Scots is less clearly
defined; but a second benefit of a Scots question in the Census
would be, precisely, that it would force the Scottish populace to confront the language question more directly than many of them, probably, ever have; and thus bring the status and identity of Scots clearly into their minds as a matter to be decided. And finally, the evidence that the central government had begun to regard Scots as a
topic worthy of official interest, if not necessarily as a language worthy of official recognition, might help to enhance its prestige and
loosen the lingering hold of the "bad English" stigma.

However, such developments must be complemented by active
efforts to rehabilitate Scots as a language in active use. It is in the
education system and the media that this rehabilitation must begin.
In some respects the situation is more favourable to a revival of
interest in the language than it has ever been. The fields of Scottish
(including Scots) literature and linguistic scholarship are admirably
healthy and active. There is now no dearth of Scots literary texts
suitable for use in schools, both primary and secondary; and a small
but growing corpus of critical studies of the major texts, and of cas-
sette recordings, is also in being and readily accessible. The Scottish
Consultative Council on the Curriculum, in assocation with all the
education authorities in Scotland, has recently published in English,
Gaelic and Scots a substantial package entitled *The Kist/a' Chiste*,
containing poems, plays, stories, pictures, comic strips, tape-record-
ings and notes and aids for teachers.[51] The material is suitable for
children of a wide range of age and ability, and should certainly help
many more teachers to encourage and support the use of Scots in
schools.

The efforts of language scholars have produced not only the mon-
umental *Scottish National Dictionary* and (still incomplete, but pro-
gressing) *Dictionary of the Older Scottish Tongue,* but as first by-prod-
ucts from those enormous projects the *Compact Scottish National
Dictionary* (a reduced-size two-volume edition of the ten-volume
original), the *Concise Scots Dictionary* (a single-volume abridgement

of the SND and the DOST, with the addition of some words not included in either of the parent works), the *Pocket Scots Dictionary* (a simplified version of the *Concise*, designed for school use), the *Scots Thesaurus* (a novel and fascinating work in which the Scots vocabulary is arranged under subject headings) and the *Concise English–Scots Dictionary* (the title is self-explanatory, and the *Dictionary* is the first academically respectable work of its kind). The recently-published *Scots School Dictionary (Scots–English/ English–Scots)* is intended for upper primary and lower secondary schools; this, along with *The Kist*, is a major advance in the encouragement of Scots among the younger generation. Further reference works, such as detailed studies of the vocabulary associated with particular fields, are in active preparation. Another recent development has been the establishment of the Scots Language Resource Centre in Perth, now a principal source of both textual and archival information and practical guidance in the Scots field.

On a more general level, developments in the fields of dialectology and sociolinguistics have made it simply impossible for any informed person to maintain the old view of Scots as a kind of bad English. In the schools and the universities (three of them at least), Scots, if only as a field of historical, literary or philological study, has now an established place. One of the most remarkable, and most encouraging, developments of the last few years has been a quite dramatic increase in the amount of attention being paid to the language in primary and secondary schools: several of the regions appointed educational advisers with the task of first ascertaining the extent to which the Scots tongue is actively used and its literature studied, and then of exploring ways in which its place in the educational system could be enhanced. Unfortunately financial and political factors have prevented this development from continuing, but not all ground has been lost.

There can be no doubt that in the nine years since this booklet's first edition much has been achieved, and the place of Scots in the national life is unquestionably stronger than it was then. Yet an important aspect of the issue has still to be fully appreciated and confronted: the fear, widely felt if not always overtly expressed, that a major revival of interest in what is distinctively Scottish, including the language, would have political implications. And indeed it would. Most, if not all, cases of language revival have been

intimately associated with political nationalist movements: there is
no pretending that an attempt to preserve or revive a language in
defiance of pressure from a dominant and foreign power can fail to
be a political issue. That it is not widely perceived as such in
Scotland – that many of us quite sincerely imagine that Scots is a
matter of purely cultural or historic interest – is a measure of the
confusion which has affected our national life for two hundred
years.[52] This confusion has led to the fatal flaw in our thinking
which has allowed the pernicious Union to continue without effective challenge long after the allegation of material benefits resulting
from it has ceased to be even a credible pretence: the lack of an
explicit and determined association between the political and the
cultural aspects of Scottish nationalism. Whether in the 1970s
adopting unedifying slogans of the "Rich Scots or Poor Britons"
order, or in the 1980s attempting to confront the crass materialism
of the Thatcher government on its own terms, or in the 1990s fight-
ing on two fronts against the pure unionism of the Conservative
party and the cosmetically-veiled unionism of Labour, the Scottish
National Party has tended to concentrate its fire in the economic
field: of course the party has a cultural policy, but arguments based
on the distinctiveness of Scottish cultural traditions have been less
than central to its strategy; and consequently an enormous reserve
of potential support, inherent in the widespread affection which the
Scots tongue and the heritage it embodies can still arouse, has gone
largely untapped. On the other side, many people think of themselves as patriotic Scots and enjoy the atmosphere of Burns suppers,
ceilidhs, folk music concerts and the like – activities which I do not
in the least mean to denigrate – and yet appear to be unable to recog-
nise the fact, or to accept its implications, that in their everyday lives
they are passively or actively supporting a socio-political system
aimed at consigning all the grounds for this patriotism to the grave-
yard of history.

The fact that the Scots language matters is an aspect of the greater
fact that the Scottish national identity matters. Every argument that
is put forward in favour of an increased use of and respect for the
language is *ipso facto* an assertion of the fact that Scotland has, and
should be proud to proclaim that it has, a distinctive national culture. On a more practical and more specific level: anyone who has
read the present book and appreciated its arguments will agree that

a desideratum is the study of Scots literary texts and the discussion of their language as a regular part of the curriculum of all school classes, and the acceptance of the language itself as a medium for teaching and classroom discussion. Another is a far greater amount of time devoted to Scots in radio and television broadcasting: plays in Scots, including recent work by contemporary writers and drama-tisations of Scottish literary classics, and discussion programmes on and in Scots, could be broadcast much more frequently than at pre-sent; and fluent native speakers of Scots could be employed as announcers, newsreaders and sports commentators. In both these fields, the fact that we have achieved some progress from a starting-point of almost nothing obscures the equally certain fact that we are still lamentably short of what any country capable and desirous of preserving its cultural heritage would consider even tolerable. If these goals were achieved, they would clearly cause our children to grow up with a stronger and more clearly-defined feeling of Scottishness than they now have, and therefore, probably, a clearer perception of the unsatisfactory state in which the Scottish nation finds itself today and an active desire to change it. This is not some-thing to fear; nor should we attempt to ignore or conceal the fact that it will, and should, be the result of the greater recognition of Scots that this book is arguing for. It would be a distortion of the facts (but one which it is very easy to imagine being perpetrated) to suggest that attempts at developing and encouraging Scottish cul-ture, including its linguistic aspects, are a mere guise for movements towards Scottish political independence: the two are in reality insep-arable, different sides of the same coin, and neither can come to full fruition without the other. Certainly some degree of cultural auto-nomy is possible, and indeed exists, in Scotland without political independence; and the example of Wales shows that in a country with even less of a distinct political status than ours it is possible to do much more than we have done to preserve the native language and culture. Conversely, the achievement of independence by the Irish Republic has not had the desired effect of rejuvenating Irish as a living language, despite the strong efforts of the government; and can hardly be said even to have led to a major efflorescence in the English-language culture of Ireland. But the fundamental fact remains that in a Scotland which is part of a unitary United Kingdom, and therefore necessarily and inescapably subject to the political and cultural domination of London, attempts to preserve, let alone develop, the native languages and their associated cultures can attain no more than limited success. Distinctive national institutions cannot flourish, though they may be kept from disappearing, in a land which is regarded, and is content to regard itself, as not a nation but a province; and conversely the citizens of Scotland will never actively demand national status for their country until they know – as at present most of them do not – that its traditions and its culture are distinctive and valuable enough to entitle it to that status.

In the first edition of this book, reference was made at this point to the ignominious failure in 1979 of the Callaghan government's scheme for a devolved Scottish assembly, the subsequent dismal period when a mood of gloom and defeatism in the national psyche allowed the social and cultural destructiveness of the Thatcher government's policies to proceed unchecked, and the growing recovery of optimism and an active desire for improvement towards the end of the decade. A new setback almost as crushing as the devolution fiasco occurred in 1992, namely the Conservative victory in the general election: the party in Scotland made retention of the incorporating Union the central issue in its campaign; and though neither this nor anything else made any important difference to the low level of its Scottish support, its victory on English votes was treated as a mandate for continuing to ignore all arguments for Scottish devolution. This might have resulted in another period of passive despondency: instead, not only has the cultural revival (of which one aspect is the steadily growing interest in Scots) flourished without interruption, but the political argument on Scotland's constitution continues to be hotly waged. The intellectual level of the debate as conducted by the politicians is often abysmally and insultingly low, and the most pathetic feature of the Scottish political scene is the splenetic and vituperative hostility expressed by the Labour party towards, not the Conservatives, but the SNP; but the temperature, if not the illumination, remains high. And a quite unmistakable feature of contemporary Scottish life is the increasingly powerful and increasingly overt commitment among the *literati* to either full or partial political autonomy. Indeed, only *one* important literary figure in Scotland, the excellent historical and political novelist Allan Massie, can be heard to argue for the incorporating Union.

The history of Scottish home rule movements in the twentieth century has been a drearily monotonous sequence of raised hopes and numbing disillusionments; but there seems at last to be evidence of real progress in the signs that the political and the cultural sides to the movement are beginning to reinforce each other, instead of operating in mutual isolation. There is no Scottish Yeats or Havel on the horizon, and active interest and participation in the literary, artistic and academic life of the country is not widespread among its leading political figures; yet the steadily increasing strength and distinctiveness – and political content – of contemporary Scottish (including Scots) letters is surely a reason for optimism.

An independent or even semi-independent Scottish government would, it is hoped, give high priority to encouraging the two native languages. Scots – both the regional dialects and the language of the mainstream national literature – could be taught, and (more importantly) *used,* in the schools as official policy. The broadcasting services, and the press, could utilise Scots on a regular, daily basis, thus ensuring that it held not a marginal but a central and integral place in the national consciousness. And now we may return to a point made earlier in the booklet. It is of course true that the boundary between Scots and English is less clear in practice than it is in theory, speakers who use a maximally "pure" Scots being rarer than those whose Scots is to a greater or lesser degree adulterated with English. But the abundant corpus of literature in a Scots much more clearly differentiated from English than is the Scots most of us speak could provide an admirable tool for re-introducing the full wealth of Scots vocabulary and idiom to the Scottish people. The common assertion – it is hardly an "argument" – that the poetry of Burns and his contemporaries or of MacDiarmid and his successors is useless to present-day readers because it is "unintelligible" is of course trivial: all poetry is unintelligible to those who have not learnt the language in which it is written. But to the extent that it deserves a reply, the obvious one is this: let us then ensure that it ceases to be unintelligible by making its language once again the common property of the poets' compatriots. There are no obstacles to this aim that could not be overcome, given the will.

Arguments ebb and flow, elections come and pass, social movements flourish or falter, books are published, read and forgotten or go on to new editions: nothing stands still, in the domain of Scots or

elsewhere. On the least flattering analysis, Scots in the last decade
has not only remained alive but has incontrovertibly strengthened
its position, both as a subject for popular discussion and, less nebu-
lously, in the educational field. This progress must be maintained.
Scots is a language, a vehicle for the thoughts and feelings of one
particular section – and, on any showing, a pretty distinctive one –
of the human family; and as such, it matters.

Notes

1. The historical existence of an analogue of King Arthur is sufficiently well established for this statement to be uncontroversial. See John Morris, *The Age of Arthur,* London 1973; and for a fascinating and very convincing attempt to identify him with a known historical figure, Geoffrey Ashe, *Kings and Queens of Early Britain*, London 1982, and *The Discovery of King Arthur*, London 1985.

2. David de Camp, "The genesis of the Old English dialects", *Language* 34, 1958, pp. 232–244.

3. The edition of *The Dream of the Rood* by Michael Swanton (Aberdeen 1970) contains a detailed description and discussion of the Ruthwell Cross, pp. 9–38.

4. For the most recent and most effective attempt at illuminating the "problem of the Picts", see Alfred P. Smyth, *Warlords and Holy Men: Scotland AD 80–1000*, London 1984, pp. 71–83.

5. See David Murison's classic study "Linguistic relationships in mediæval Scotland", in G. W. S. Barrow, ed., *The Scottish Tradition: Essays in honour of R. G. Cant*, Edinburgh 1974, pp. 71–83.

6. For discussion of the language names see J. D. McClure, "Scottis, Inglis, Suddroun: language labels and language attitudes", in R. J. Lyall and F. Riddy, eds., *Proceedings of the Third International Conference on Scottish Language and Literature (Mediaeval and Renaissance)*, Stirling/Glasgow 1981, pp. 52–69.

7. See Mairi Robinson, "Language choice in the Reformation: the Scots Confession of 1560", in J. D. McClure, ed., *Scotland and the Lowland Tongue: Essays on the Language and Literature of Lowland Scotland in honour of David D. Murison*, Aberdeen 1983, pp. 59–78.

8. For a recent detailed discussion of this phenomenon, see Jenny Wormald, "James VI and James I: two kings or one?" in *History* 1983, pp.187–209.

9. In the introduction to *The Minstrelsy of the Scottish Border*.

10. Dublin 1932; revised edition 1972.

11. "The good old Scots tongue: does Scots have an identity?", in *Minority Languages Today*, E. Haugen, J. D. McClure and D. S. Thomson, eds., Edinburgh 1981. (Revised edition 1996)

12. H. Kloss, *Die Entwicklung neuer germanischer Kultursprachen seit 1800* (second edition), Düsseldorf 1978, section 1.1.1.

13. The most readily accessible account of Scots as pronounced in different regions is in the Introduction to the *Scottish National Dictionary*. Vol. 3 of the *Linguistic Atlas of Scotland* contains much more detailed

information but the presentation is perhaps too technical for a general readership.

14   See H. C. Wyld, *Studies in English Rhymes from Surrey to Pope*, New York 1965, pp.70-75, and for more detailed discussion E. J. Dobson, *English Pronunciation 1500-1700*, Oxford 1968, Vol. II, pp. 576–585 and 810–826 (the case of *oi* is here shown to be very complex, but the simple statement in the text is valid as far as it goes).

15   J. Sherzer, ed., *The Origin and Diversification of Language*, Chicago 1971, pp. 271–284.

16   The most complete and systematic description so far published of the grammar of any form of Scots is the relevant section in C. MacAfee, *Varieties of English Around the World: Glasgow*, Amsterdam 1984.

17   E. K. Brown and M. Millar, "Auxiliary verbs in Edinburgh speech", *Transactions of the Philological Society* 1980, pp. 81–135; see also "Aspects of Scottish English syntax" by J. Miller and E. K. Brown, *English World-wide* 3, 1982, pp. 3–17.

18   "Orpheus and Eurydice", l.414; "Braid Claith", ll.1-2 Cf. A. J. Aitken, "Bad Scots: some superstitions about Scots speech", *Scottish Language* 1, 1982, pp.30–44.

19   For discussion see J. D. McClure, "The debate on Scots orthography", in Manfred Görlach, ed., *Focus on Scotland: Varieties of English Around the World* General Series 5, Amsterdam 1985, pp 203–210; for the most recent set of practical suggestions, see "Recommendations for writers in Scots", *Lallans* 24, 1985, pp. 18-20.

20   James Hogg, *The Three Perils of Man*, chap.18.

21   David Purves, *The Wurfs o Merlin's Craig*, in *Lallans* 23, 1984, pp. 6–8.

22   See P. Hume Brown, *Early Travellers in Scotland*, 1891, pp. 39–55.

23   Keith, "An Address in Scotch on the Decay of that Language", printed in Andrew Shirrefs, *Poems Chiefly in the Scottish Dialect*, Edinburgh 1790, xxiv-xxvii; Robertson, "On the Decadence of the Scots Language, Manners and Customs", *Poems*, Dundee 1878, pp. 42-62.

24   See A. Feitsma, "Interlingual communication Dutch-Frisian, a model for Scotland?", D. Strauss and H. W. Drescher, eds., *Scottish Language and Literature, Mediaeval and Renaissance, Fourth International Conference 1984*, Proceedings, Frankfurt 1986, pp. 55–62.

25   "Scots is not alone: further comparative considerations", in J.-J. Blanchot and C. Graf, eds., *Actes du 2ᵉ Colloque de Langue et de Littérature Écossaises (Moyen Age et Renaissance)*, Strasbourg 1978, pp. 80-97.

26   For a comprehensive study, see K. Bitterling, *Der Wortschatz von Barbours Bruce*, Berlin 1970.

27   The association of poets with kings' reigns is of course in most cases no more than a mnemonic device, but the coincidence of a literary renaissance with the coming to power of James I is not accidental. See Louise O. Fradenburg, "The Scottish Chaucer", in Lyall and Riddy, eds.,

op.cit., pp.177-190, and J. MacQueen, "Poetry: James I to Henryson", in R. D. S. Jack, ed., The History of Scottish Literature Vol.1: *Origins to 1660*, Aberdeen 1988, pp. 55–72.

28 And totally forgotten in our own time until the researches of William Donaldson, embodied in his fascinating books *Popular Literature in Victorian Scotland*, Aberdeen 1986, and *The Language of the People*, Aberdeen 1989.

29 J. D. McClure et al.,"Our ain leid? The predicament o a Scots writer", in *English World-wide* 2, 1981 pp. 3–28; M. P. McDiarmid *et al.*,"The Scots-English Round-Table discussion: `Scots: its development and present conditions, – potential modes of its future': three `Scots contributions', in Strauss and Drescher, eds., *op.cit.*, pp. 93–99.

30 See the classic study by W. Craigie, "The earliest records of the Scottish tongue", *Scottish Historical Review* 22, 1924, pp. 61–67.

31 For a detailed study see J. D. McClure, "What Scots owes to Gaelic", *Scottish Language* 5, 1986, pp.85–98.

32 *Cf.* V. E. Durkacz, *The Decline of the Celtic Languages*, Edinburgh 1983.

33 See Bitterling, *op.cit.*

34 For a detailed study see David D. Murison, "The Dutch element in the vocabulary of Scots", in A J Aitken *et al.*, eds., *Edinburgh Studies in English and Scots*, Edinburgh 1971, pp.159–176. No study as comprehensive as those cited for Gaelic and Dutch as yet exists for the other foreign elements in the Scots vocabulary, but see also David Murison's short but informative article "Norse Influence in Scots", *Lallans* 13, 1979, pp. 31–34.

35 See McClure, "Scottis, Inglis, Suddroun", in Lyall and Riddy, eds., *op. cit.*

36 "Duncan Gray", l. 39.

37 "Gairmscoile", in *Penny Wheep*, 1926.

38 "The Flyting of Dunbar and Kennedie", ll. 241–2.

39 *The Bevellers*, Edinburgh 1974, p. 50.

40 For a discussion of MacDiarmid's use of the expressive force of Scots words in an altogether more serious context, see David Daiches, *God and the Poets,* Oxford 1984, Chapter 9.

41 For a substantial recent collection of proverbs see David Buchan, *Scottish Tradition*, London 1984, pp. 182–190; and for an anthology with sources, discussion and perceptive comment, see David D. Murison, *Scots Saws*, Edinburgh 1981.

42 *Cf.*, for example, George Steiner, *After Babel*, Oxford 1975, p. 470: "As it spreads across the earth, `international English' is like a thin wash, marvellously fluid, but without adequate base".

43 On Pennsylvania Dutch, see Kloss, *op. cit.*, pp. 125–133, and references therein; the origins of the Mennonite and Hutterite communities are briefly discussed in P. E. Keller, *The German Language,* London

1978, p.345; on Cajun see Patrick Griolet, *Mots de Louisiane*, Acta Universitatis Gothoburgensis XXX, Paris 1986.

44 On Argentina see Garbhan MacAoidh, "Gaidhlig ann an Argentina", *Gairm* 1974; on Nova Scotia, a convenient summary is the entry by Sister Margaret MacDonell in D. S. Thomson, ed., *The Companion to Gaelic Scotland*, Oxford 1983, pp. 214–7.

45 For a brief discussion see the review of Vol.1 of the *Linguistic Atlas of Scotland* by Raven McDavid, *Journal of English Linguistics* 12, 1978, pp.76–82, and "English in New Zealand" by Laurie Bauer in Vol. 5 of the *Cambridge History of the English Language* (ed. Robert Burchfield) Cambridge University Press 1994, p. 407.

46 See Nancy C. Dorian, *Language Death*, Philadelphia 1981, for a full account of this phenomenon. This book is a study of the moribund Gaelic dialect of East Sutherland, but as a major contribution to the literature on language relationships it should be read by all who are interested in the topic.

47 *Cf.* E. Haugen, "Language fragmentation in Scandinavia: revolt of the minorities", in Haugen *et al.*,eds., *op. cit.*

48 G. E. Davie, *The Democratic Intellect: Scotland and her Universities in the Nineteenth Century*, Edinburgh 1961, p. 31; quoted in P. H. Scott, *In Bed with an Elephant*, Saltire Pamphlets New Series 7, Edinburgh 1985, p. 25; a book whose arguments are particularly relevant to the present discussion.

49 James Beattie, *Scotticisms arranged in Alphabetical Order, designed to correct Improprieties of Speech and Writing*, Edinburgh 1787.

50 Iseabail Macleod and Aonghas Mac Neacaill, *Scotland, a Linguistic Double Helix*, European Bureau for Lesser Used Languages, Dublin and Brussels 1995

51 Scottish Consultative Committee on the Curriculum, *The Kist/a' Chiste*, Nelson Blackie, London 1996.

52 For further discussion see J. D. McClure, "The Pinkerton Syndrome", *Chapman* 41, 1985, pp. 2–8.

Further Reading

THE MOST AUTHORITATIVE and accessible descriptions of Scots are to be found in the Introductions to *The Scottish National Dictionary* and *The Concise Scots Dictionary*. Besides these and the references in the text and the notes, the following works, listed chronologically, can be recommended to readers interested in enhancing their knowledge and understanding of the language.

James Wilson, *Lowland Scotch*, Oxford 1915. An early scholarly study of the pronunciation, grammar and vocabulary of the dialect of Strathearn in Perthshire. Includes an interesting collection of proverbs and idioms, and lists of words classed under such headings as "food", "clothes", "domestic animals", etc. Wilson's invented spelling is at first somewhat forbidding, but is an ingenious and accurate representation of the sounds of the dialect.

W Grant and J. Main Dixon, *A Manual of Modern Scots,* Cambridge 1921. Indicates pronunciation by phonetic transcription. Includes, besides accounts of phonology and grammar, several texts chosen to illustrate different dialects.

Angus McIntosh, *Introduction to a Survey of Scottish Dialects, Edinburgh* 1961. An account of the scope, aims and methods of modern dialectology, with particular reference to the work of the Linguistic Survey of Scotland. Very useful as a corrective to the notion that Scots exists only in texts and glossaries.

A. J. Aitken, ed., *Lowland Scots*, Edinburgh 1973, reprinted 1979. Four papers providing respectively a summary history of Scots, accounts of it as a literary language in the mediaeval and the modern periods, and a discussion of the modern spoken language and the theoretical approach to its study. An essential introductory text.

J. D. McClure, ed., *The Scots Language in Education,* Aberdeen 1975. Six papers focusing principally on the social status of Scots and its place in the educational system past and present.

A. J. Aitken and T. McArthur, eds., *Languages of Scotland*, Edinburgh 1979. Deals with both Gaelic and Scots: on the latter, contains discussions of its historical relations with English and its use in modern poetry. Also includes papers on Scottish English: its history and status, and a detailed account of its pronunciation.

73

The following three items are Numbers 2, 3 and 4 in the Association for Scottish Literary Studies' series of Occasional Papers.

David D Murison, *The Guid Scots Tongue*, Edinburgh 1977. Short, readable, but very informative and wide-ranging. Includes numerous samples of texts.

William Graham, *The Scots Word Book*, Edinburgh 1975, revised 1980. The account of Scots pronunciation is presented in an unscholarly fashion, but the lists of English–Scots and Scots–English equivalents are a fund of interesting information.

Billy Kay, *Scots: the Mither Tongue,* Edinburgh 1986. The most complete account of the subject for a popular readership. Lively, partisan (an nane the waur o that), informative: a particularly useful contribution is the section comparing the status of Scots to that of other European minority languages.

Also:

J. D. McClure, *Scots and its Literature*, Amsterdam 1995. A selection of the author's previously published articles, with revisions and updatings, discussing many aspects of Scots including its use in some canonical literary texts.

Some Saltire Publications

Geoffrey Barrow, *Robert the Bruce and the Scottish Identity*   0 85411 027 5   £1.00
I. B. Cowan, *Mary Queen of Scots*   0 85411 037 2   £2.50
David Stevenson, *The Covenanters*   0 85411 042 9   £2.95
Kenneth MacKinnon, *Gaelic: a Past and Future Prospect*   0 85411 047 X   £7.95
Meston, Sellars and Cooper, *The Scottish Legal Tradition* (new edition)   0 85411 045 3   £5.99
William Neill, *Tales frae the Odyssey o Homer owreset intil Scots*   0 85411 049 6   £7.99
William Ferguson, *Scotland's Relations with England: a Survey to 1707*   0 85411 058 5   £12.99
Paul Scott, *Andrew Fletcher and the Treaty of Union*   0 85411 057 7   £12.99
Paul Scott, *Walter Scott and Scotland*   0 85411 056 9   £7.99
David Daiches, *Robert Burns the Poet*   0 85411 060 7   £12.99
David Stevenson, *Highland Warrior: Alasdair MacColla and the Civil Wars*   0 85411 059 3   £12.99
David Daiches et al., *The Scottish Enlightenment 1730-1790: a Hotbed of Genius*   0 85411 069 0   £14.99
John Sibbald Gibson, *Edinburgh in the '45: Bonnie Prince Charlie at Holyroodhouse*   0 85411 067 4   £7.99
Thorbjörn Campbell, *Standing Witnesses: an Illustrated Guide to the Scottish Covenanters*   0 85411 061 5   £16.99

Saltire New Poetry
Raymond Vettese, *A Keen New Air*   0 85411 063 1   £7.99

Forthcoming Editions
David Purves, *Grammar and Usage in Scots*   0 85411 068 2
Rosalind Mitchison (ed.), *Why Scots History Matters* (new and enlarged edition)   0 85411 070 4
Ian Grimble, *The World of Rob Donn* (new edition)   0 85411 062 3

Membership details from:
Saltire Society, 9 Fountain Close, High Street, Edinburgh EH1 1TF